REGULATION IN ACTION

REGULATION IN ACTION
The Health Professions Council
Fitness to Practise Hearing
of Dr Malcolm Cross—Analysis,
History, and Comment

Janet Haney

KARNAC

First published in 2012 by
Karnac Books Ltd
118 Finchley Road
London NW3 5HT

British Library Cataloguing in Publication Data

A C.I.P. for this book is available from the British Library

ISBN-13: 978-1-85575-777-6

Typeset by Vikatan Publishing Solutions (P) Ltd., Chennai, India

Printed in Great Britain

www.karnacbooks.com

For Bea Low

CONTENTS

ACKNOWLEDGEMENTS

The work that led to this book began as preparation for the conversations preliminary to the "rally of the impossible professions" (ipnosis.postle.net/pages/UN-CONHome.htm) staged in London by the New Lacanian School in September 2008. Around that time a group of people from different varieties of practice (life coach, counsellor, therapist, psychoanalyst, etc.) formed a network called "The Alliance for Counselling and Psychotherapy". These two events provided the momentum and channels for the information and ideas that allowed my work to take shape. There are many people who were important along the way, all of them I would like to thank, and in particular: Paul Atkinson, Bernard Burgoyne, Evonne Cameron, George Freeman, Nick Galwey, Stephen Gee, Penny Georgiou, Guy Gladstone, Richard Gombrich, Paul Gordon, John Haney, Richard House, Darian Leader, Roger Litten, Douglas McFadzean, Jennifer Maidman, Michael Power, Denis Postle, Werner Prall, Andy Rogers, Andrew Samuels, Bruce Scott, Marilyn Strathern, and Peter Wood.

ABOUT THE AUTHOR

Janet Haney obtained her PhD in organizational sociology at Trent Polytechnic, Nottingham in 1987, and her Masters in Psychoanalytic Studies from Brunel University in 1995. She works in London as a practitioner and a freelance researcher.

FOREWORD

This book documents a professional misconduct case that came before the Health Professions Council (HPC) in the United Kingdom in March 2010. It will interest many psychotherapists who have been campaigning vigorously against state regulation. This occupational group has been unusually active among professional groups affected by legislation in lobbying politicians and journalists, holding rallies and generally making noise. Some organizations (the PsyReg group) even obtained permission for judicial review by the High Court of the capacity of the HPC to regulate the field.

In addition to being a Lacanian analyst, Janet Haney (née Low) has a doctorate in social science and also belongs to the amateur theatre world. This book might make a good play at the Royal Court. It uses an entertaining story, revealed through a legal hearing, as a vehicle for making an argument about how we have slipped by degrees into a form of tyranny in Britain through ill-conceived regulation. It is also a biographical account of someone whose life has been affected by neo-liberalism, and provides a good example of the value of seeing our private troubles as public issues (Mills, 1959). While working on a research project at Imperial College's School of Medicine, she found that "knowledge and truth (along with the idea that genuine research entails, by definition, impartiality) were being sidelined, and that market research and scientific management were more the order of the day" (p. 25). After making a career move to psychoanalysis, she found that similar changes were taking place there.

There are many Janet Haneys around, in the sense of educated people with a commitment to professional practice in different fields, who are feeling alienated at present, as the nature of the British state is slowly being subjected to increasing economic rationalism. Such people may feel empowered by this book; there is value in giving a critical voice to the experience.

Through serendipity, Haney happened to live in South London near the building in which the public hearings of the Health Professions Council were conducted. She started to observe these hearings, and to write a blog reporting on what was discussed by the committee tasked with establishing the regulation (www. hpcwatchdog. blogspot.com/), but also the other public documents circulating about the issue, and relevant meetings. This was done with a great deal of persistence, wit and intelligence over a couple of years, and became a well-documented account of the evolution of a bureaucracy, but also a series of essayistic thoughts about professional work and values, and the role of government in regulating the professions. More broadly, the blog can be read as a puzzled response from one thinking person to what has happened to Britain in the past twenty years. Although it does not consider academic literatures in great depth, it is interspersed with discussions of political scientists and sociologists who have written about bureaucracy, documentaries made by avant-garde film makers about these issues, and excerpts from theatrical plays being staged in London that seemed relevant to the deliberations of the HPC.

This book is written in a similar way to the blog, although it has a narrower focus. It describes, and offers reflections, on a professional disciplinary hearing conducted by the HPC. This is presented as an example of a case that should never have been heard, and it is suggested in the last chapter that far too many trivial cases are being pursued at great expense because the bureaucracy that exists has been set up on a false premise. What Janet Haney conveys is the resulting Kafkaesque and comedic nature of the proceedings. Since they were established with the supposed aim of saving money, tribunals have been criticized for not having proper rules and procedures, and for resulting in unfairness. This was certainly true of this hearing. Janet Haney does not, however, simply make the point intellectually. She invites the reader to share her visceral distaste for the whole system by presenting lengthy extracts, puncturing the pomposity and vacuousness of the quasi-legal language, and making us question the legitimacy of the whole enterprise. At the end of the book, we learn that the HPC secured its power through legislation, and then secondary legislation that was never properly debated. She also criticizes lawyers for their tacit support at various stages, suggesting that they benefit from this form of regulation and hearings of this kind.

In addition to describing the routine work of this regulatory agency from a critical perspective, Janet Haney is also interested in where regulation comes from, and why professionals are now said to be unable to manage their own affairs. She asks why there seems little interest in the subject from most university academics. During the 1990s, Power (1997) and O'Neill (2002) wrote powerful books about the rise of auditing and quality assurance in Britain, but most academics are silent on these issues. Haney notes in relation to the erosion of academic freedom that:

> the unwillingness of the vast majority of this country's academics to acknowledge the existence of the tragedy (an online petition set up by young scholars attracted only 500 signatures), to even begin to publicly address this betrayal of a core cultural heritage, appears to have become a fact of life. (p. 26)

In fact, the position is even worse in two respects. Firstly, university research is itself subject to a particularly pointless form of assessment, currently called the Research Excellence Framework, that purports to measure the quality of publications but has the unintended consequence of increasing volume at the expense of quality. Critical researchers, as much as anyone else, are engaged in a ruthless competition for survival, as funds for research are concentrated in elite universities. This book might not even count for the Research Excellence Framework since it has not been published by a university press and does not contain scholarly discussion of relevant academic literatures. Nor should one be naïve enough to believe that attempts to reward "impact" support lively, critical studies about social institutions. What the government-approved assessors mean by "impact" is responsible research that contributes to improving the performance of the economy and public services, often by establishing even more regulation.

Secondly, despite their own negative experiences of bureaucracy, many social scientists have become part of the quality assurance industry. In universities, there are particular pressures to conduct "useful" research for government, which often means contributing to some regulatory programme. There are also influential research centres on regulation in our top universities. Inevitably, these produce favourable accounts of regulation, even though some researchers recognize there are unintended consequences (Haines, 2011). The tendency of these academics and intellectuals to support regulation, however, cannot simply be laid at the feet of politicians keen to shape and manipulate intellectuals. One should also recognize that there have always been academics who have supported the state in its struggle against other interest groups, and who have benefited from resulting expansion of their own power. Today, those concerned about the regulation of professionals may find themselves supporting, without recognizing any contradiction, the call to regulate the banks or emissions trading. In each case, however, there is considerable evidence that modern forms of regulation have very little effect, other than creating opportunities for regulators.

This, however, still leaves the question as to what intellectual objections can be made against quality assurance, as represented in this book by the HPC. Haney mainly expresses a skepticism for bureaucracy, auditing, and managerialism, and offers some interesting thoughts on why state regulation is damaging:

> When regulation is split off and handed to people who are asked to know nothing of the practice, a lacuna is created. In such a case no reason, no body of knowledge, no evidence, no discrete idea or philosophy underpins the "system" of regulation—these are the conditions in which political and economic power can grow unchecked. (p. 9)

This is a similar argument to that made by Durkheim (1952), Carr-Saunders and Wilson (1933), and later writers such as Freidson (2001), about the importance of the professions in protecting the public against excessive state power. Against that, one can argue that disciplinary hearings held by the HPC are still public and that the regulators do not directly tell professionals how to deliver their services (though a detailed analysis of the way that training courses are affected in the long term might reveal an effect yet undiscussed). But Haney and other critics would counter that those implicated in the state machinery have attempted to shape work and values in many occupational fields. A good example would be university teaching, in which managers and educational experts have successfully changed practices, and how we understand standards, despite some resistance from those committed to traditional values.

As a sociologist, it is difficult to present much good news to any-one who has become subject to state regulation or to anyone concerned about the growing influence of the state on our everyday professional and personal lives. According to IMF figures, during the period 2000 to 2009, state expenditure as a proportion of gross national product in Britain rose from 36.6% to 47.2%. One big growth area has been reg-ulation. To give one example, Ofsted the organization that inspects schools and ranks them into league tables, was founded in the early 1990s. Previously, teachers and school heads obtained informal advice and support from friendly inspectors. But Ofsted has developed into a massive, judgmental bureaucracy. Today, many teachers take sick leave to avoid inspections. Others expend tremendous effort to win the stars one can see proudly displayed outside schools, just as if they them-selves were children being rewarded in a classroom.

There is, of course, no evidence whatsoever that inspection or even the quality of leadership improves school achievement over a long period of time. This has much more to do with investment decisions made by local and central government. To the best of my knowledge, there has been no independent scrutiny of Ofsted based on observing inspections (remarkable given its own commitment to inspections and evaluation). Even today, no politician can question Ofsted without appearing to be soft on educational standards.

Durkheim might view the recent history of the state in Britain as an extreme, pathological case. It is a country that is, after all, known for bureaucracy, and a slow and idiosyncratic legal system. In a book about quality assurance (Travers, 2007), I found that managers in a police force portrayed multiple layers of regulation, and professionals spoke about their struggles with forms and administrative procedures, in terms reminiscent of a postwar Ealing comedy. This book portrays Britain in a harsher light: as a country in which unaccountable groups can achieve power, and make people's lives a misery, through playing on our fears about professional misconduct. Haney even suggests that there is something rather base in pursuing such cases:

> It is as if the process has been specially constructed as a machine for destroying knowledge and spreading ill will. There can be little doubt that the process feeds feelings of vengeance and even hatred. (p. 180)

One cannot really blame the problem on a failure of governance in Britain. IMF figures also show government spending expanding in every developed country during the twentieth century so that it accounts for half of GDP. At the same time, modern management believes almost as a matter of faith that performance can be continually improved. This is why regulatory agencies, including the HPC, are constantly searching for ways to measure the quality of professional work. As many critics have argued, this is often highly problematic, since applying expert knowledge requires the exercise of judgment. Nevertheless, psychotherapists along with other occupations have been asked to accept what often makes no intellectual sense in order to satisfy regulatory agencies. The result has been a lowering of morale among motivated professionals across the public sector.

There are many who get on and achieve the equivalent of Ofsted stars, either through cynical compliance or because they have convinced themselves of the value of the measures. Others feel disempowered, and become alienated by what Power describes as "rituals of verification". As Haney points out, there is no evidence that any of these quality assurance regimes have raised quality. To give an example, those who inflicted the Research Quality Framework on universities believe that it has raised quality because more papers in good journals are published. They are unable to see the weakness of this argument.

Perhaps the best thing about *Regulation in Action* is that it does not advance a critique at a speculative level, but describes one example in some detail. If you suspect that something is deeply wrong in the relationship between the modern state and civil society, and that there is a kind of colonization of professional work taking place, you will find this book both informative and empowering. In contrast to most current academic studies, there is no equivocation. This book makes a persuasive case that Britain can save itself a lot of trouble, and gain the chance to reinvest millions of pounds into productive, intelligent work, through abolishing the HPC and returning to work-based regulation.

© Max Travers
School of Sociology and Social Work,
University of Tasmania, Australia

CHAPTER ONE

Some steps that led to this book

This book is quite particular and rather unusual. Most of it is a transcript of the fitness to practise case of a psychologist and HPC Council Member, Dr Malcolm Cross. I have chosen to present this transcription (made available under the law that created the Health Professions Council, henceforth the HPC) in order to allow people to grasp the reality of the new regulatory framework that now exists in this country. Very few people, even amongst those directly affected, seem to know what the framework is based on, nor how it arose. Much of the problem is that the new regulation is based on quite different assumptions from those we are accustomed to, and it is the arbitrary change in these underlying assumptions that make it difficult to grasp what's going on. During the course of my research into this problem, Dr Cross's fitness to practise case came forward. It occurred to me that the transcription of this case would provide the perfect material to reveal the nature of what is actually going on. The case itself reads rather like a soap opera, and has a curiously compelling character. It is quite fun to read. However, this is not the level at which the real information exists. The case is presented in order to show the mechanisms and procedures that are put into play in the name of "public protection". Dr Cross himself is not the primary concern of this book, but a useful and unavoidable vehicle for it. I have topped and tailed the transcript with an introduction and conclusion. In Chapter One, I have brought together some threads that make up the backdrop to the case, and which help to make sense of what has happened. The concluding chapter also includes other information arising from my wider research into the HPC, which helps to show how the single case presented here is part of a wider pattern of chaos. I hope that it helps to frame the material and to prompt more people to act.

1959: CPSM—one register for eight professions

On 20 November 1959, *The Times* newspaper announced the impending creation of the Council for Professions Supplementary to Medicine (CPSM). The paper's political correspondent reported:

> Eight new professional bodies with the general function of promoting high standards of education and professional conduct, and each with its investigating and disciplinary committees, will be set up under the terms of the Professions Supplementary to Medicine Bill which was published yesterday ... *Each profession will have a board to regulate professional conduct.* Their first duty will be to maintain a register of all persons qualified for the profession and to approve training courses, qualifications and training institutions and will have power to cancel registration in cases of misconduct. [emphasis added]

Ten days later, on 30 November 1959, the bill was due for its second reading in the House of Commons, and *The Times* responded to the occasion by publishing a leader comment and a letter of dissent from the speech therapists (Morley, Court & Tuck, 1959). The leader article looked forward to a law to rid the country of charlatans, while the letter argued the need to avoid registration in order to protect and pursue its academic credentials: two rather different points of view on the function and effects of statutory power. The Conservative Minister of Health (Mr Derek Walker-Smith) opened the reading in the House of Commons. In his introduction he explained that the bill was an attempt to bring together eight different professions *without common organization* and that this would be tricky and time-consuming. There were also, he said, many interests to consider, including those of the medical profession under whom these eight callings were to perform their "supplementary" functions (chiropody, radiography, remedial gymnastics, etc.).

> We intend that the Bill should make it possible to distinguish people *eligible for employment in the public service*—health, welfare, school health and education—but I should like to make it clear that the Bill does not seek to ban the employment of other than registered people … Similarly, the Bill *does not prohibit private practice by unregistered people* but merely protects the title "State Registered". [emphasis added]

The government was grappling with how to employ people in the NHS and clearly thought that a register, which people could opt into, was a practical, if not entirely logical, solution. It was down to the speech and language therapists to spell out the implications this had for the field of knowledge that supported a practice.

Reading through the Hansard transcript, it is possible to hear the astonishment of the politicians at the reluctance of the speech therapists to take this "gift". But one can also read how they eventually conceded to the demands and did not insist that the speech therapists enter the CPSM. The following excerpt from Hansard from a speech by Dr Barnett Stross, Labour MP for Stoke on Trent, reveals something of the relation between politics to the professions at the time:

> There again, the article in *The Times*—not the letter but the leader—is quite right. The speech therapists can do all this and still have state registration and do nothing but gain by it. If, however, as a last resort, they refuse, *we cannot help it. They will be free if they insist upon it.* I can only say that I hope they will listen to what some of us in this House are saying and to what we shall say in Committee and realise that they can do nothing but gain. We cannot see how they could possibly lose. [emphasis added]

Depending on where they were sitting, everyone had a different point of view (Scott, 1998), but the arguments from the speech therapists prevailed, and they were eventually to enter a statutory register forty years later when the HPC took over from the CPSM in 2001.

The pressure to create a new organization arose out of the problems experienced in the management of the CPSM. The UK Health Departments (of which by now there were four due to devolution) commissioned a report in 1996 by JM Consultants—"Report of a Review of the Professions Supplementary to Medicine Act (1960)". This report does not so much explain what had changed but manifests some of the signs of the change as well.

1996: The JM Consultants report

The JM report notes that much had changed in British society since the 1960s (education policy reform, NHS reform, the increased numbers of professions and members) but it did not remark on any of the main currents of health problems faced by British society at the time or indeed on anything else. Instead, JM kept it local and consulted with interested parties to discover that almost everyone was unhappy with the CPSM: "*Most support our view* that the problems are now so severe that new legislation is required. However, there are differing views on the direction which this should take" (p. 3, emphasis added). Although the problems outlined in the report *all point to tensions arising from the idea of regulating multiple professions with a single regulatory organization*—a possible cause of the problems—the solution JM came up with was, astonishingly, more of the same.

The report dismisses the dissenting voice by insinuating that it is a self-interested voice, or one too bogged down in details to see the "bigger picture". Thankfully, *The Times Higher Education Supplement* (in 2000) was not so partial, so we can learn that:

> Many chiropodists, radiographers and others in the remaining ten professions supplementary to medicine say the new arrangements will undermine their attempts to maintain standards and protect the public.
>
> "They will be able to put on my tombstone that I fought to the bitter end," says Raymon Ariori, chair of the chiropodist board of the CPSM.
>
> "Only a madman or a fool could possibly believe that the new arrangements will help patients," he says.
>
> He argues that the new council—which will establish common procedures for the different professions—will undermine the status of individual professions and will make it easier for universities to get approval for poor-quality courses. (Sanders, 4 February 2000)

Nevertheless, JM stuck to the political vision and strategy, which pressed on regardless. When considering the increasing number of people who opted out of registration, a number that was supposed to dwindle away to nothing as a result of a natural choice from the public, JM acknowledged that it had in fact increased. But rather than read this as a sign of dissatisfaction with the CPSM regime, JM assumed it was a call for stricter control by the state.

In 1959 the politicians had recognized that bringing eight different practices together in one organization would be both unnatural and difficult and required caution and care. In 1996 this consideration had disappeared. Instead of seeing that a specialized approach might maintain independent, creative, responsive, and responsible conduct across the practices then covered by the CPSM, JM recommended weakening the powers of the professions by removing the powers of the boards. It also recommended increasing the power of the central council by decreasing the number of professionals and increasing lay membership. And in a final move against experience and knowledge they opted for "efficiency of scale" by opening the possibility for unlimited numbers of new professions to be brought into the structure.

All this weakens the mechanisms of self-regulation. The new proposals attack the basis upon which a process of rational and *enlightened regulation* takes place. That is, the proposals favour a system based on the power of politics and economics, rather than the power of reason in relation to particular practical reality. This, of course, is a giant step backwards, and cannot be considered a sign of progress.

Enlightened regulation belongs to the community that is implicated in the practice and the creation and transmission of knowledge that supports the practice. By grounding the regulation amidst the knowledge and experience of a practice it is possible to temper the rise of political power within the system. That is, political power must take its chances with the actual contexts and problems faced by the practitioner within a system of laws and a consideration of ethics. When regulation is split off and handed to people who are asked to know nothing of the practice, a lacuna is created. In such a case no reason, no body of knowledge, no evidence, no discrete idea or philosophy underpins the system of "regulation"—these are the conditions in which political and economic power can grow unchecked.

In an adjacent field, that known as the study of audit culture, a similar lacuna has been noted where we see the bizarre consequence of people spending valuable time proving to their managers and auditors that they are running a quality service, rather than *actually* running a quality service (see for example, Cooper, 2001; Power, 1994, 1997, 2009; Strathern, 2000; Travers, 2007). The structure of this problem serves a "double whammy". First, valuable time is taken away from doing the job while practitioners attend to tick-box form filling, and second, valuable headspace is taken up with a form of thinking that has nothing to do with the actual job in question. It is possible to see how this in itself will undermine the structures of reason and control that are necessary for the proper regulation of a practice—the careful attention to what is going on by people who are experienced and responsible for the practice. The collapse in this attention is likely to lead to problems in the practice. Ironically these problems, whose causes are structural and out of sight, then get taken up by the new regulators who propose it as "evidence" for the need for increased state control.

John Major's government had no obvious plans for actioning this report. But the year after the publication of the JM report, New Labour was swept to power with a majority of 418 seats (sixty-six percent) over 165 (twenty-six percent) for the Conservatives and forty-six (seven percent) for the Liberal Democrats.

1997: The impact of New Labour

One of the first items on the agenda of any new government is usually the setting out of its plans to reform the NHS, and the 1999 Health Act did just that. Section 60 of the act includes words that empower "Her Majesty" by "Order in Council" "… to make provision to modify the regulation of any profession so far as appears to be necessary or expedient for the purpose of securing or improving the regulation of the profession or the services which they provide".

So while the act might have gone through all the usual steps afforded by the democratic tradition, this section of the act was left deliberately vague and provided an opportunity for the government to take executive action at some future date. Executive action was duly taken a couple of years later, with the introduction of the secondary legislation—a statutory instrument, the Health Professions Order 2001 (henceforth HPO 2001). It has been noted that in an attempt to pass record levels of legislation this Labour Government introduced cut-off times on debates, and made use of increasing levels of secondary instruments which required no general debate.

The arrival of HPO 2001 also marked the exit of a private member's bill seeking to establish a General Psychotherapy Council, which had been introduced by Liberal Democrat peer Lord John Alderdice. This rather quiet coup marked the change from traditional statutory regulation (where power is passed to an organization responsible for the practice), to the new regulation, which requires the creation of a new regulator that does not know about the practice.

In the meantime the public inquiries into Dr Harold Shipman, tried and found guilty of murdering many of his patients (Smith, 2001), and the Bristol Royal Infirmary, concerning mortality rates among infants who underwent cardiac surgery there (Kennedy, Howard, Jarman & Mclean, 2001), were giving a particular and pernicious backdrop of support to the government's programme of change in the NHS. Although these two inquiries were quite different from each other, the political atmosphere fused them together and they both became fuel for the idea, much amplified by politicians and the press, that "doctors" as a set of people could not be trusted and needed to be brought under state control. We will come back to this shortly.

This gave John Hutton's speech the sensational backdrop he needed to get away with a surprisingly aggressive attitude against the integrity of the professions. He introduced HPO 2001 as a means of dealing with charlatans, adding:

> The greater the access to independent practitioners, the stronger the case for regulation because those in managed services such as the National Health Service are more likely to be subject to a higher degree of quality control.

He had made the assumption that it is NHS control mechanisms that guarantee practitioner quality. Not only does this make huge and probably imaginary assumptions about the cohesion and stability of the NHS, it is also little more than a parody of Taylorist factory management, which supposes that skilled labour has already been eradicated (see Braverman's seminal *Labor and Monopoly Capitalism: The Degradation of Work in the Twentieth Century*, 1976). When Hutton spoke of the chiropodists—decent, law-abiding citizens, with a history of good practice despite the lack of a university degree—he said:

> I have received representations from practitioners *in the unregulated sector* saying that the order unfairly discriminates against them, but it does not. [emphasis added]

Not only does this view of regulation misrepresent them as being unregulated (that particular misrepresentation will be repeated regularly from now on) but Hutton also appears to assume that he knows best. Although this is similar to the position held by Dr Barnett Stross in 1959, it is also utterly different. Being right has turned into something less pleasant. He went on:

> I assure the Committee that we are not bashing the *unregulated* sector.

Repeating the point that those with a different view are an unruly lot ("unregulated") and flatly denying that he is doing something that his previous words clearly indicate to be his main purpose, he then concludes:

> We want to be open and fair. We are not approaching the task in a spirit of hostility or discriminating against those with unregistered qualifications.

In fact, the order as written implied that anyone without a degree, no matter what their track record to date, would, in the event of enactment, find themselves criminalized if they continued to see their patients. The next speaker, Dr Evan Harris (Liberal Democrat MP for Oxford West and Abingdon), frames his opposition to Hutton diplomatically:

> I do not necessarily disagree with the Minister, but he has now said twice that he is not trying to discriminate against the unregistered sector. He might have seen the same representations that I have, arguing that state-registered chiropodists who never took a degree— even those who trained many years ago and have since retired— should not have to go down the pathway of further qualifications or tests. In a sense, that is discriminatory. Will he comment on that?

Hutton replies:

> We have tried to find a compromise and consensus, but they have eluded us.

Without elaborating on the nature of the effort, or on the reason for the failure, Hutton simply hammers home the idea that the public is in danger from *unregulated* practitioners who put themselves, in his view, beyond the reach of discussion.

The vote in the House of Commons was undertaken separately from the debate in committee and on another day: 28 November 2001. The results can only reflect the dimensions of the political consensus of the day, and not the result of reasoned debate: 292 supporting (seventy-two percent), 113 opposing (twenty-eight percent).

A fortnight later, on 13 December at 9.31 p.m., the debate was opened in the House of Lords by Lord Hunt, who also chose to emphasize the need for a punitive role for the HPC:

> The council will have wider powers to deal with individuals who present unacceptable risks to patients as set out at Articles 22 to 33 of each order. It will have powers to deal with registrants whose fitness to practise is impaired, whether through ill health, lack of competence, or misconduct. That will be a big improvement on the current limited powers of the CPSM, which is able to deal only with infamous conduct in a professional respect and has only one option for action, which is striking off.

His introduction was followed by the then Opposition spokesman for health, Earl Howe, who proposed an amendment to the order which sought to ease the situation for those facing disenfranchisement, and to increase the range of representation on the new committees. He raised the point that a

> large group of non-state registered practitioners of chiropody and podiatry are far from happy with the order

and gave a succinct presentation of the situation without implying that society was in danger of cheats and scoundrels. He pointed to practical issues:

> All of a sudden we shall be faced with the prospect that a substantial number of chiropodists and podiatrists who are doing important and valuable work will no longer be available to look after their patients. A large decrease in chiropodist numbers

will put added pressure on an area of the NHS that is already over-burdened. [Furthermore] The Society of Chiropodists and Podiatrists, which represents the state-registered sector, is worried that there will not be adequate representation for each profession on the HPC ... [That] the HPC will be dominated by the state-registered sector; the independent sector will have no representation on it whatsoever.

Baroness Dean (a Labour peer) opposed him, following her party's line:

Certainly, the provisions within the order for closure of title—as a lay person would express it—will prevent those without appropriate qualifications *parading* as titled practitioners. [emphasis added]

The attitude of the government is clear. Today's professional class appears rather like the old unions, something to be controlled and contained.

2001: The Bristol Royal Infirmary Inquiry (BRII)

The BRII report was published in July 2001 and recommended the creation of what was to become the Council for Regulating Health Professionals (CRHP), now known as the Council for Health Regulatory Excellence (CHRE) and soon to be changed to something more suitable for the current political climate (perhaps the Professional Standards Authority). The CRHP was established as the regulator of the regulators and shared the discourse of transparency and protection that also characterizes the HPC. On 30 October 2008, the BBC broadcast Ann Alexander's programme "Do Public Inquiries Work?" It opened with shocking headlines from the Shipman tragedy and a quote from the chairman of that inquiry (Dame Janet Smith) but immediately went on to focus on a very different matter—the BRII. The link between the two inquiries (Bristol and Shipman) is weak and serves mainly to insinuate that the goings-on at the BRII were as dark and sinister as Dr Shipman's mind. This, however, is completely untrue. In fact, the link between the two cases is Alexander herself, who represented the families of those murdered by Harold Shipman and won the right to a public inquiry.

The problem at the Bristol Royal Infirmary was summarized by the BRII as follows:

> The story of the paediatric cardiac surgical service in Bristol is not an account of bad people. Nor is it an account of people who did not care, nor of people who wilfully harmed patients. It is an account of people who cared greatly about human suffering, and were dedicated and well-motivated ... It is an account of healthcare professionals working in Bristol who were victims of a combination of circumstances which *owed as much to general failings in the NHS at the time* than to any individual failing. Despite their manifest good intentions and long hours of dedicated work, there were failures on occasion in the care provided to very sick children. [emphasis added, p. 1]

This spectacular lack of any specific disaster leaves us in the dark as to the origins of the BRII, but one thread in Alexander's programme is perhaps the closest we can get to a credible reason for all the fuss. Michaela Willis originally accepted her tiny son's death as having been a risk that was difficult to avoid—her new baby had been seriously ill and the operation had been a critical one; he died aged just seven days old. However, as time passed and general discontent with the situation at the hospital began to receive publicity, she naturally found herself wanting to know more about the case of her son. Unfortunately, her requests for information proved too much for the hospital administrators, whose lack of forthcomingness Mrs Willis took as a personal rebuff. This, in turn, provoked her into taking further action.

What happened next was fuelled in part by a series of articles that appeared in *Private Eye* in 1992 (14 February, 27 March, 8 May, 3 July, 9 October, 20 November). GP Dr Phil Hammond, the (anonymous at the time) author of these pieces, had been a medical student in the late 1980s and had found the experience so traumatic—as he said later in an interview published in the *New Statesman*—that he had had to transform it into a comedy act in order to speak publicly about it. He and his friend Tony Gardner went to the Edinburgh Festival in 1990 as "Struck Off and Die" and this, in turn, resulted in an invitation to write for *Private Eye* ("by 1992 I started taking my anger out in *Private Eye*"; quoted from "Killing Fields and Other Doctors' Tales", *New Statesman*, 23 July 2001). Michaela Willis, however, was neither angry nor inhibited, but straightforwardly aggrieved to have the question of her baby's death re-opened in a way she found mystifying. "We never wanted to blame anybody, we actually just wanted to find out what had happened", she said. In so saying, she was asking a clear and perfectly rational question that needed to be addressed: what actually happened in the cases of the babies that did not survive? This particular question was never posed either by the inquiry, or by Ann Alexander's programme. In fact, it appears to have been vetoed at a political level before the inquiry even began. Asking this question would almost certainly have done much to explain the individual tragedies and could also have been a good way to isolate the factors that actually affected the outcomes. In the end, however, it was, perhaps, political considerations that won the argument and a public inquiry was launched which, despite its own declared wishes, ended up scapegoating two medical professionals and the hospital's chief executive (formerly also a medic).

Chapter 11 of the BRII is titled "The Expression of Concerns by Individuals and Reactions to Those Concerns". It begins by noting how difficult it was to establish any order from the accounts of what had happened at the hospital between 1984 and 1992. It immerses the reader in the complexity of acronyms, people, roles and services that exist in the name of the NHS and that spill over into associated institutions (including universities). The relationships between all these various groups are, to say the least, complex. Anything resembling clarity is nowhere to be found even at the end of the chapter. The pervasive vagueness stemming from the unwillingness of anyone to say anything specific about anything in particular creates a gap in the text that then becomes the problem. The inquiry had been set to work without a specific remit, and in the writing of the report, and in the orientation of the questions, the vagueness became an attribute of the hospital itself, which in turn became "the problem" that the report seeks to explain. What are never properly addressed are the political moves that created turmoil in the structures of the NHS.

Chapter 12 opens by restating the theme of the report—that "to a very great extent, the flaws and failures of Bristol were within the hospital, its organisation and culture, and within the wider NHS". This is, in essence, a very, very vague (not to mention extremely oblique) reference to the fundamental changes—among them the establishment of the new NHS Trusts—that were being introduced by the government at the time. Having thus implied that the problems at the hospital could be explained by a closer scrutiny of politics and organization, the inquiry then proceeded simply to ignore those two factors and instead singled out a series of named individuals for criticism.

How did the BRII get off the ground? The new government was looking for an opening to make major changes to the NHS. Alexander's radio broadcast reports how Frank Dobson (the Secretary of State for Health at the time) remembers meeting some of the bereaved parents. At the end of the meeting, one of the mothers said: "Do you mind if I kiss you?" Dobson didn't mind, and the mother then told him: "You are the first official person who's actually sat down and listened to what we had to say". His comment on this was: "... if someone in an official position had sat down a year or two before, had actually sat down and listened to what the parents had to say, there might never have *been* an inquiry, nor a scandal in Bristol". The question remains why no one did listen to them—presumably those in power preferred to listen to the political "change-makers" who were making a great deal of noise at the time. Dobson may have had a point, but others in Blair's inner circle immediately spotted an opportunity to make political hay. Dobson's meeting turned out, in fact, to be crucial in the run-up to the decision to stage a public inquiry.

The BRII cost £14 million and lasted three years (from October 1998 to July 2001). It produced a 1,200 report, along with several thousand pages of annexes. Max Travers summarized his reading of the report in his book *The New Bureaucracy: Quality Assurance and Its Critics* (2007): "Whether or not this was the intention, the whole document can be read as a sustained argument for doctors and ... other professionals to be subject to greater regulation ... The thrust of the argument is that the main failing at Bristol, and throughout the NHS, was that there was no proper system for monitoring quality ... Although the report states that it is concerned with improving systems as opposed to criticising groups or individuals, it is difficult to escape the conclusion that the main villain was the medical profession for resisting quality assurance ... One gets the sense of professional groups resisting this form of regulation successfully over many years, but equally so the determination of government to introduce ... practices of measuring and assuring quality ... It is also apparent that the beneficiaries in this process are not simply patients, but the organisations established to measure and monitor quality, and more generally quality assurance as a new occupation". (p. 28)

This is an important consideration to grasp, pointing as it does to a structure that is otherwise occluded. The existence of a set of people (e.g., Doctors) who have worked and studied to achieve a level of competence in a practice that other people might need to access from time to time is generally held to be valuable in societal terms. It recognizes the will of people to get on and do something worthwhile without there needing to be a law forcing them to do it. The underlying assumption is that there are certain conditions where men and women can be trusted to keep themselves and each other harmless unless and until proved guilty of doing the opposite—not the other way round. This assumption contributes to an elaborate network of relationships that make up a civil society and mediates the power of the state. It helps to protect individual subjects from the sudden intrusion of state power into the mundane details of their lives.

The BRII report was published in July 2001, just a few weeks before HPO 2001 entered the parliamentary process. Although there is nothing in particular linking those two occurrences—i.e., it wasn't especially marked out to contribute to the debate about the HPC—the political electricity surely runs back and forth between them, along with the message not only that doctors couldn't be trusted to sort it out themselves but that NHS management (especially those who had once themselves been medics) would probably also collude against the patient.

2003: A box of tricks—the magic of advertising

In the summer of 2010, when the HPC were having to work hard to maintain their interests in capturing Counselling and Psychotherapy, chairwoman Anna van der Gaag was invited to write an article for Psychotherapist, the journal of the United Kingdom Council for Psychotherapy (UKCP); Issue 46, Autumn 2010. In it she says that the underlying principles of the HPC are "mutual trust" and "light touch" and that the fitness to practise (FTP) process is based on the principles of "restorative justice". These comments must be read against the HPC's 2004 advertising campaign and against the actual FTP processes, of which we will see one glaring example shortly. I had attempted to discover from the minutes of HPC meetings the process whereby the decision to go ahead with the campaign was taken. The committee papers I received contained no information whatsoever to shed any light on the question (Council 13 May 2004; Communications Committee 5 July 2004)—a deficiency the HPC explained as arising from the fact that its minutes were "not standardized" at that point. However, the papers contained reference of a report presented to the HPC dated 28 June 2004 by Box of Tricks—the advertising agency whose services the HPC had retained—and this does contain other information that is helpful to us here.

According to the report, Box of Tricks had convened a series of focus groups between January and June 2003 covering around one hundred members of the public. At the beginning of the day, the participants stated that they had high expectations of health professions but thought they often received poor healthcare because the NHS was under-resourced and over-burdened. They did not believe their poor treatment was due to inconsistencies in training or to incompetence on the part of health professionals, who, they said, were doing an admirable job in difficult circumstances. The participants believed that all health professionals were fully qualified and competent, and the vast majority of them took it for granted that the NHS or other employers would carry out the necessary checks, and that this was not a job for the patient to undertake (Topline Report, 1 July 2004, pp. 3–4, attachment to HPC Communications Committee of July 2005).

As the day progressed, the group leaders must surely have succeeded in sowing seeds of doubt because, by the end of the day, the forum had changed its mind. The report notes that people had "come to the conclusion" that patients were too trusting, that only "regulation within healthcare should achieve high standards", that poor standards could lead to death, and that there was confusion over whose responsibility it was to maintain standards. The Topline Report notes that by this time in the meeting people had forgotten about the responsibility of the employer and were instead wondering whether the responsibility should be with the unions, the government or independent regulatory bodies. It is difficult to believe that citizens would so easily give up their opinions unless they had been manipulated into doing so.

As a result, then, of the management of the group, the participants had, apparently, become more and more convinced that only HPC regulation could save them from being harmed by shoddy practitioners in old-boy networks. As the report draws to a close, we hear forum members comment "that just knowing the HPC exists will encourage patients to … complain", and participants even say (lapsing, quite inexplicably, into the language of marketing) that they believe that the "HPC can maximise the effectiveness of their communications [by] establishing an easily recognisable brand". The report "concludes" that "The HPC's role, remit and aims are largely endorsed by patients and the wider public".

How disappointing that this piece of work was not rejected by the members of the HPC Council and its chair, Anna van der Gaag. Instead, the advertising campaign that then went ahead showed little evidence of either "trusting" or indeed of a "light touch".

2004: The HPC advertising campaign

The HPC launched its first major advertising campaign in 2004. Four of the five posters from this campaign were framed and hung on the wall in a corridor at the HPC's headquarters until shortly after I wrote about them on hpcwatchdog.blogspot.com (19 November 2008). That they counted as art to be displayed in a corridor leading to the committee rooms where the HPC's FTP hearings were held surely tells us something about the organization's ideological complexion.

---

1. A picture of a man dressed up as Dr McCoy from Star Trek on the bridge of the USS Enterprise. The headline: "You can trust me ... I'm the real McCoy". The small print: "Who can say if a health professional is genuine? The fact is that any genuine health professional must shortly be registered with the Health Professions Council. The HPC is the statutory UK body appointed to regulate and maintain the standards of 12 health professions. To use one of the professional titles below, pretenders have until July 8th 2005 to meet our criteria. If they prove to be genuine, they can join over 150,000 professionals already on our register. Anything less and they're on a different planet".
2. A picture of a woman with a very, very, very long nose and rouged cheeks, looking a little like Pinocchio. The words on a poster behind her: "The Muscle Management Consultancy PH.one.Y". The voice bubble: "Professional titles? To tell you the truth they're a thing of the past!" The small print: "Who can say if a health professional is genuine? Sometimes letters after a name don't prove anything. Anyone who is a genuine health professional with genuine qualifications must shortly be registered with the Health Professions Council ... after that, telling lies becomes an offence."
3. A picture of a woman under a theatrical spotlight, wearing something in very large check. The speech bubble: "Tonight, Matthew, I'm going to be ... a Health Professional!" The small print: "Who can

say if a health professional is genuine? You don't become qualified overnight. All genuine health professionals must shortly be registered with the Health Professions Council ... after that, they are acting beyond the law."

4. A picture of a man in a white coat and a swimming hat with goggles on his forehead standing in front of a wall of certificates. The speech bubble: "Fitness to Practise? I can show you hundreds of certificates". He is holding up a certificate dating from his days at school and proclaiming him "Swimming Champion" in 1978. The small print: "Some qualifications aren't worth the paper they're written on. All genuine health professionals must soon be registered with the Health Professions Council to prove their credentials. ... All true professionals have until 8 July 2005 to become registered with us or lose the right to use titles listed below. Those that lie will be in deep water".

Liars, fakers, jokers, and pretenders—all of which smacked of a scare campaign. The barely coded message was that the public was in danger from the professional class (see O'Neill, 2002 for an elaboration of the way this ideology actively undermines trust). Although there is no evidence to support the idea, it was given the full investment needed to turn it into a serious advertising campaign. The inspiration behind the campaign visuals might be traced to the front cover of Ian Kennedy's *The Unmasking of Medicine* (1981) (Kennedy was an academic law lecturer at the LSE at the time). It was the text of his 1980 Reith Lectures. The artwork displayed the familiar and reassuring image of a doctor wearing a mask while conducting an operation. The juxtaposition of this picture with the highly polemical title of the book, however, effectively re-characterized an otherwise purely utilitarian item of specialized clothing as an instrument of deception. Kennedy's book was an attack on the right of doctors to pronounce on matters such as (among others) homosexuality, abortion, madness, and death. While it is true that these matters are too important to be left solely to people with medical degrees, the tenor of the book essentially ignored the practicalities and reality of the situation. Rather than grappling with this, Kennedy chose to launch a polemic against doctors.

"Just as the 1980s saw the crippling of the trade unions, so the 1990s and the 2000s bear witness to a concerted effort to weaken the so-called professions" (Leader, 2008, p. 206). Ian Kennedy's idea, first aired in the 1980s was taken up again when New Labour came to power in 1997. Lord Irvine, Tony Blair's "pupil master" at the Bar, telephoned

Ian Kennedy (a personal friend) one night to see if he would agree to chair the BRII. He said yes.

2007: The White Paper and the politics of unhappiness

On 7 February 2007, Lord Alderdice asked the government what progress it had made on the statutory registration of psychology, psychotherapy, and counselling since stopping his own bill (House of Lords, Hansard). He reminded the government that all the major organizations in psychology, psychotherapy, and counselling had unambiguously rejected the HPC as a regulator for their field.

Baroness Pitkeathley (Labour Peer) was the second to speak that evening. She introduced herself as a "fan" of the psy field and applauded the government's intention to regulate via the HPC, saying that she hoped it would "take the mystery out and put the regulation in". Perhaps it was this rather chilling attitude that was soon to win her the position as Chair to the CRHP.

Conservative spokesman for health, Earl Howe, in his turn went through the British Psychological Society's objections to the HPC in detail, and urged the government, "even at this late stage, to leave open the possibility of an independent statutory regulator for psychologists, psychotherapists and counsellors" when the White Paper is published. "That", he said, "is the formula most likely to produce a sense of ownership among the professions. We may have waited many years to reach a resolution of these very difficult issues, but whatever resolution is reached has to work".

Two weeks later the White Paper was published ("Trust, Assurance, and Safety—The Regulation of Health Professionals in the 21st Century") which proposed that "… psychotherapists and counsellors will be regulated by the Health Professions Council, following the Council's rigorous process of assessing their regulatory needs and ensuring that its system is capable of accommodating them". Psychologists had been separated out from this group and were pushed through first as a separate profession—each section of the HPC register is supposed to refer to a unified and coherent practice. Statements against the HPC subsequently vanished from the BPS website.

In October 2007, the Labour government announced its plans to invest £170 million to make "talking therapies" increasingly accessible in the NHS. This launched the Increasing Access to Psychological Therapies (IAPT) scheme, which looked good at first glance but was in fact tangled up with some rather indeterminate ideas about happiness and was even more vague about the kind of evidence which could be collected to measure and then augment it (see for example, Leader's article in the *Guardian* newspaper, 2007; and my letter to the BACP magazine *Therapy Today*, Low, 2007). Politics seemed to have become caught up in a search for miracles, and those in charge of the organisations in "talking therapies" seemed not to mind the attention that happiness was suddenly getting. Not only did the proposed investment effectively promise well-paid jobs for individual practitioners, but it also anticipated a government-controlled market for particular types of training. The implication was that if you could get your type of talking therapy recognized on the register, your future as a trainer for this workforce was guaranteed. Consequently, many people were extremely keen to go along with the politics, so keen, in fact, that they turned a blind eye to the quid pro quo of the deal—the profession would have to give up its responsibility for control of its practice and accept HPC regulation. As I've already argued, this amounts to giving up the link between practical responsibility and rational or enlightened practice.

On 24 April 2008, the BBC current affairs programme *Analysis* broadcast an episode titled "War of the Professions". The presenter, Alison Wolf, opened the programme by claiming that the government was actively undermining the power of the professions by introducing independent regulators. She presented two positions in relation to this policy. On the one hand, the professionals presented their knowledge and experience as the best qualification for regulating their practice. On the other, managers and politicians argued that professionals would inevitably make decisions in their own favour rather than in the best interests of the patients—the managers and politicians feared that the professionals had become much too powerful and that they were using that power for their own personal advancement. On the one hand, then, there is an appeal to knowledge and ethics, on the other to fear and greed. No scrutiny of the ethics and motives of management and politicians was offered.

On 1 July 2009, Parliament delegated power, via the Health Care Associated Practices (Miscellaneous Amendments) No 2 Order, 2008, to the HPC to take over the registers of practitioner psychologists from the BPS and to undertake the regulation of those practitioners.

2008: Capturing counselling and psychotherapy

When the HPC called for ideas about regulating counselling and psychotherapy (in the summer of 2008), it was against this backdrop. The sudden change of direction with the psychologists was evidence that political ideas were pushing an ideological agenda that had yet to be subjected to a sustained critique. It was this that prompted me to act.

Before becoming involved with psychoanalysis, I had been a sociological researcher in higher education. My trajectory began as Mrs Thatcher started to dismantle the socio-economic structures she loathed, and my PhD thesis tracked the changes in personnel and industrial-relations management at British Telecom as it was being "deregulated" and sold off to the private sector in the interests, apparently, of "decentralization". Ten years later, I was recording the privatization of Thames Water as the Arthur Andersen consultancy were demonstrating how to use new computerized technology to capture knowledge from the operations of water and sewage treatment plants with a view to quantifying and monetizing them. This project, amusingly enough in the context of privatization, was referred to as "centralization". Another ten years passed and I was engaged by Imperial College's School of Medicine ostensibly to protect "continuity of care" for patients of GPs and psychiatrists. It was all too apparent, however, that knowledge and truth (along with the idea that genuine research entails, by definition, impartiality) were being sidelined, and that market research and scientific management were more the order of the day.

This unexpected and disappointing revelation requires some background information and explanation. While Richard Gombrich was Oxford University's Boden Professor of Sanskrit, he made a speech to the Graduate Institute of Policy Studies (GRIPS) in Tokyo in 2000 ("British Higher Education Policy in the Last Twenty Years: The Murder of a Profession"). This remains a very important point of orientation for anyone interested in the structural shifts initiated by Thatcherism. Gombrich tracked the political interventions that have so badly damaged the structures that once supported the British tradition of academic freedom—and, by implication, of respect for learning and dedication to truth—exemplified, until recently, and in particular, by Oxford and

Cambridge. A slow trickle of articles (Eagleton, 2011; Fish, 2010; Head, 2011) and books (Docherty, 2008; Gerstman & Streb, 2006; Naylor, 2007; Russell, 1993) adds weight to this critique. Yet the unwillingness of the vast majority of this country's academics to acknowledge the existence of the tragedy (an online petition set up by young scholars attracted only 500 signatures), to even begin to publicly address this betrayal of a core cultural heritage, appears to have become a fact of life. Despite the existence of a growing literature tracking the intellectual and philosophical vacuity of audit culture (Cooper, 2001; King & Moutsou, 2010; Power, 1994, 1997; Strathern, 2000; Travers, 2007), the apparent popularity of this cultural paradigm shift remains undiminished and— even more unbelievably—uncontested. What, then, explains this?

Some critics see fear as a factor (Voruz, 2009); others suggest that people positively enjoy participating in these structures of falsehood, cherishing the sense of order that it creates, relishing the material rewards, devoting themselves to the constant production of so called "proof" that their work is of genuine value (Power, 1997).

These are all signs that what we take for granted as the underlying structure of British higher education and the concomitant structure of research has in fact changed or collapsed. Knowledge, once a product of the search for truth, is becoming little more than the "quantifiable" outcome of a process concerned not with truth, but with economic profit.

What to do?

Because I lived quite close to the HPC's offices, because I had spent many years as a sociological researcher and because my intellectual history had already allowed me to begin to make at least a little sense of the radical changes that had taken place in this country since the 1980s, I decided to go along to the HPC and to take advantage of its much-vaunted policy of "transparency" and turn my expeditions into fieldwork. I began to attend the HPC's offices regularly (November 2008) and to observe its FTP hearings, as well as HPC Council and other meetings, and to publish my field notes on a blog so that other people who might be interested in what was happening could readily access the information. More than a year into this process, an FTP hearing was posted on the HPC website that promised to condense the questions into one neat case and to provide a possible vehicle for widening the debate.

The case related to HPC Council member Dr Malcolm Cross, a psychologist. His position of responsibility at the HPC gave his case a much higher profile than those of practitioners in the HPC's FTP process who preferred not to have their names more widely circulated. Dr Cross was not only a beneficiary of the HPC but also one of its advocates. More importantly, in my opinion, he was actually in a position to be able to do something about the possible deficiencies of the HPC if he could bring himself to acknowledge that something was in fact wrong with it.

This book is an analysis of Malcolm Cross's FTP case. The main body of the text is drawn from the transcript of his hearing, which is available to anyone who requests it from the HPC.

CHAPTER TWO

The FTP case begins

D
r Cross's FTP case entered the public domain in February 2010, when a notice was posted on the HPC website four weeks in advance of the hearing. The allegation was set out in three points, the first of which was divided into seven separate instances amounting to the allegation of misconduct, leading, in turn, to the statement that "by reason of that misconduct your fitness to practise is impaired". A colleague of mine spotted the case on the list of upcoming hearings and remarked on the strangeness of the allegation (Scott, 2009). I recognized the name of the registrant immediately—Dr Malcolm Cross, a recently appointed member of the new, redefined and reduced HPC Council. It was only seven months since the "practitioner psychologists" had entered the HPC register. Since HPC cases tend to take about 18 months to come to hearing, I calculated that the case must have originated quite some time ago or that it was being rushed through—probably because of the status of the defendant. Either way, to appoint someone to the new HPC Council only to then discover he was subject to a complaint raises some difficult questions.

At first glance it seems to suggest either that the recruitment process was flawed or that Dr Cross had tried to cover something up (which seemed highly unlikely). It seemed more possible to me that the mere fact of the HPC's arrival on the scene might well explain the existence of the complaint. There are three angles to consider here. First, it is possible that the offence would not have been deemed serious enough to warrant full-scale treatment in the regulatory climate that existed prior to the creation of the HPC. Second, the impact of the HPC on the field may have created some unrest and conflict when one of its members gained access to the HPC Council. Third, as noted in the Box of Tricks forum, the mere presence of the HPC (together with a strong advertising campaign) would generate complaints. To be sure, appointments to the Council have micro-political ramifications. They do not reflect a profession's view of the excellence of a particular person—nor is there a vote amongst practitioners, large-scale or small (as had been the case in the CPSM). There is no procedure required from the BPS to push someone onto the Council. Indeed, they have nothing to do with it at all. But the power accorded this person in virtue of his membership of the Council will not be uninteresting to anyone in a profession where questions of theory and practice have traditionally been subject to radical contention.

Whichever way you look at it, this case was interesting and I considered it important to attend the hearing.

There were only four in the audience that day. We had each reported to the receptionist and received yellow (for the public) or red (for the press) tags and been asked to wait in the adjacent waiting room. This area deserves a brief comment. Something about it reminded me of the special chamber found in a submarine or a movie spaceship—one that can be locked from both sides as if to prevent a sort of contamination from occurring. It indicates that what happens within the ship would be seriously jeopardized if something from the outside were allowed to seep in. Next, we were escorted through the security doors and led down the corridor to where the registrant, the lawyers and the administrators were already in their places, in the large, bright, modern room allocated for the hearing.

Sometimes this room is used for HPC Council and other committee meetings, and it is set out in much the same way as it would be then. The tables are arranged in a large oblong, leaving a large empty space in the middle of the room. On the table are nameplates marking the seating arrangements of the main actors. There is no visible cue to help the public to understand the formal position each player will hold—except of course for the technical equipment used by the stenographer.

Apart from this, there is no clue as to the distribution of power; the way the room is organized presents everyone as if they are on the same level—everyone, at least at this stage, *appears* to be equal.

At one end of the room, near the door, two rows of chairs are set against the wall for the audience—we'll call this end the "auditorium" to get an orientation: downstage, the stenographer sits with her back to the audience. In a kind of reversed theatrical metaphor, she will transcribe all the words spoken during the hearing, turning it into a script. This script is put into the public domain by the HPC, and forms the basis of this book. The chair next to her is empty until the first witness is called.

As we approached the room, we could glimpse the actors through the full-length glass walls of the room. The person who had shepherded us down the corridor handed us over at the door to the hearings officer, who invited us to sit in the chairs in the far corner of the room. This seemed a little over-diligent, and I could only imagine that she was anticipating a crowd of late arrivals whom she would then be able to seat easily nearer the door. None of us obeyed this instruction however, being much more interested in finding a seat that would afford a decent view of the proceedings.

The Panel entered. This highly theatrical act transformed the atmosphere. Silence fell. The Panel is made up of three people, only one of whom is an HPC registrant from the same part of the register as the person against whom a complaint has been brought. Of the other two, one may be from another HPC-regulated profession, and at least one (i.e., maybe two) will be a lay member (*not* an HPC registrant). The Panel acts as one, rising together, sitting together, entering, and exiting the room together. They take up their seats near the door, at stage left.

Good morning everyone …

This gives the stenographer her cue for what will become nearly two days of typing.

I am Clare Reggiori, the Panel Chair, and like my fellow Panel members, I am independent of the HPC.

I had been to a few hearings at the HPC, but I had never heard a chair declare her independence before. I knew the Panel members were obliged to reach an independent decision and had learned that they are called *partners* of the HPC. An HPC partner is not a legal owner in the sense that the John Lewis partners are, but is someone selected, trained, appraised and paid by the HPC (around £310 per day plus expenses). For comparison, here is the way another Panel Chair introduced the proceedings, at the hearing of a speech and language therapist:

> Good morning, ladies and gentlemen. I would like to open this Health Professions Council Conduct and Competence hearing by introducing the Panel. On my right is Miss Lesley Hawksworth, a lay partner; on my left is Mr Martin Duckworth, a speech and language therapist; and my name is Trevor Williams. I am a lay partner with the HPC and I am chairing the hearing today. Perhaps we can go round the room and my colleagues can introduce themselves. (5 January 2009)

It occurred to me that Miss Reggiori had been specially appointed from another regulatory body in recognition of the registrant's membership of the HPC Council. Whatever the reason, her statement was odd and created ambiguity. The gentleman to her left said:

> I am Richard Birkin. I am not quite independent; I am the Registrant Panel member.

The puzzle remained when the lady to her right said:

> I am Jillian Alderwick. I am *the* lay member of the Panel.

Although we were only about a dozen people, the rules of procedure seemed to prohibit questions, and as no one else asked for clarification, the anomaly remained unexplained. Later, I wrote to the CEO of the HPC to ask him to clarify. He still hasn't answered.

The Chair then invited the registrant, Dr Cross, sitting opposite the Panel, to state his name. This was also a slight departure from the routine I'd observed before, which typically goes anti-clockwise around the room, thus ending with the registrant. Following her instruction, Malcolm Cross stated his name, and then his lawyer, sitting to his left, declared himself (Mr Tyme). Next to him was the HPC solicitor, Ms Kemp. These three are seated stage right (i.e., house left, from the audience point of view) down the long side of the table, facing the Panel. The way they have arranged themselves, however, clearly shows that, although they may share a certain status, they are absolutely not a unit. There was a clear gap between the two lawyers, indicating the two sides in this contest. On the other side, however, the three people making up the Panel were arranged evenly, with the Chair in the centre.

Upstage (in the most commanding position from the audience's point of view), facing the audience, the Hearings Officer, Ms Akua Dwomoh-Bonsu, sits at the right hand of the Legal Assessor, Mr Russen, who takes the opportunity to make a short speech:

> I am Simon Russen. I am the Legal Assessor and I am afraid I have to be a bit longer than everybody else because I have to say what my job is and what my job is not.

You would be forgiven for thinking that Mr Russen is the judge of this court; he is certainly sitting at the head of the table, capable of upstaging everyone, and enjoying the best view of the whole room. In one way, he is the judge, but in another, he is not. In this regulatory environment, the function of the judge has been carved up and redistributed. Most of his power seems to have been given over to the Panel, but they regularly defer to him throughout the proceedings as if unsure of their ground. At times it is more helpful to think of the Panel as the jury, though its role is more complicated and its composition is quite different. The Panel is empowered to act as judge, jury and inquisitor (both for the prosecution and for the defence). With the function of the judge thus fractured, Mr Russen and the Panel must find a way to work together without this becoming apparent. When called to act, the Panel often makes use of the Legal Assessor's expertise, and at times this dependency can seem extreme and gives a fractured character to the proceedings. However, it is not for this reason that Mr Russen has decided that he needs to say quite a lot about the nature of his role; his long intervention here is not typical of other hearings, and must have been provoked by something particular in today's case, probably the status of the registrant:

> First, I am not a member of the Panel, so that when it comes to decision-making, I do not participate in those decisions. All decisions are for the Panel and the Panel alone. I am a lawyer, and my primary job is to ensure that these proceedings are conducted

properly in the sense that the correct procedure is followed and the right law applied.

It is not at all clear which laws will apply here: Dr Cross has neither broken a law nor breached a contract, so what function does the Legal Assessor in fact perform? The law in question at the HPC is the statutory law that brought the HPC into existence (powers delegated to committees, etc.) and that limits the use of the titles under which practitioners may carry on their trade.

> I can, of course, seek to help other people with those issues of procedural law if they wish me to do so.

Mr Russen is the highest-paid professional in the room (around £600 per day) but his expertise is legal. This hearing does not belong to lawyers in the way it does in a regular court. The hearings are ostensibly about the various practices that are linked to medicine and largely conducted in the NHS and should, by a certain logic, belong to the practice in question. The *laws* that are in question at an FTP hearing should be the laws of *practice*. These kind of laws should be governed by theory, argument, practice, and the tradition that the field in question has built up, knows, and is responsible for. Since the creation of the HPC, the practice is now supposed to be governed by standards that have been written up by committees (known as Professional Liaison Groups) that are dispersed once the job is done. It is these standards to which the solicitors are supposed to refer as they build their fitness to practice case. It is these standards, therefore, that are supposed to become conduits of the law. The relation between the law and the business of the hearing is, it seems to me, tenuous.

The responsibility of the court is dispersed and obscured; this has the effect of undermining the knowledge that should be at play. The logic appears to support the virtue of innocence, but in practice is nothing more than ignorance. In this way the only people who are able to build up any experience over time here are the HPC lawyers and the Legal Assessors. These people are here time after time, case after case. The Panels don't work together as teams over time and the defending solicitors come and go without building up experience.

> As to how I go about doing my job, if the Panel are in this room then so too will be Dr Cross and Mr Tyme and they will hear what I am asked and how I reply to it and that ensures that the lady

> sitting over there makes a record of it and you have an opportunity
> to have a say about it.

This information appeared at first to be directed to the world at large, of which we in the audience were the tangible representatives. He might easily have addressed us directly and used the speech to set the stage nicely for everyone present. However, midway through the sentence, it becomes clear that he is actually speaking directly to Dr Cross. By making Dr Cross and his lawyer both the subject and the object of his address, Mr Russen simultaneously alienates the audience and doubles the importance of Dr Cross, who is now both audience and participant in the show. It is as if the whole thing is some elaborate induction training in the mode of a reality TV show.

> But the rules do allow Panels to ask for advice when they are in
> their private room. That is permitted. But if it happens in that way,
> when we are next in here, I will [when back in the hearing room]
> summarise the request that has been made of me and summarise
> how I have replied to it, again, to ensure that it is recorded and you
> have an opportunity to comment on the advice I have given.

He presents himself as subject to a kind of natural justice wherein the representative of the accused may challenge anything that seems prejudicial to his or her client. On the surface, this seems fair and equal, yet it ignores the differential in position, as reflected, for example, in function and in remuneration. It also requires that everyone be familiar with the way this kind of "law" works, bold enough to challenge a senior member of the profession, and astute enough not to mistake the Legal Assessor for a judge. From what I have seen and read of these hearings, this does not seem to be very well established as a practice even though it is now nearly ten years old.

The scene appears to be a radical new way of acting, yet I'm not sure that any of the participants are quite up to the demands that are being made of them. The function of the judge, as we have already noted, appears to be distributed over several people, and assumes a kind of levelling. Yet something still needs to be raised above all others in order to make the thing work. The ambiguity bogs down the action.

Mr Russen continues:

> And, finally, it is often the case that the Panel ask Legal Assessors to
> help them with the drafting of the decisions that they make along

the way. That is permissible, but if it happens, two things: one, it is important that you should remember that it is only with the wording of the decision the Panel will already have arrived at, and, two, I will disclose the fact that I have had a hand in the drafting of it.

This, now, is quite clear. The Panel—the appointed representatives of common sense, are supposed to be the ones able to cut through the chaos and establish the truth, pass judgement, administer justice. But they are unable to do so without the legal advice. It appears to be Mr Russen's *way of speaking* that is valuable—it is the *wording*. This editorial advice, however, must then submit itself to the scrutiny of the court, in case … what? It seems to be in case he is tempted to take personal pleasure in the power that would otherwise pertain to his position. He is presenting himself as someone who needs to be kept in check, yet he purports to be the one to keep the others in check. There is something of Lewis Carroll at play in the creation of this, it seems.

For comparison, here is the introductory statement made by the Legal Assessor in another case:

> THE LEGAL ASSESSOR: My name is Angela Hughes and I am the legal assessor. My role is to advise the panel on law and procedure and to ensure that proceedings are conducted fairly and properly. I am independent of the panel and any advice I give to the panel will be placed on the record. I may be asked to assist the panel with the structuring of the decision. If I do so, I will only be asked to join the panel once it has reached its decision. I do not participate in the decision-making process itself.

All the information is presented here in a simpler, shorter statement. It is also very succinctly put in Article 40 of HPO 2001, where just a few sentences lay out the framework ("The legal assessors, when advising the Council or any of its committees, to do so in the presence of the parties or their representatives or, where advice is given in private, requiring the parties to be notified of the advice tendered by the legal assessors … [this does] not apply to advice given by a legal assessor in respect of the drafting of a decision …")

Once Mr Russen has finished, the Panel Chair regains control. She addresses the registrant directly and explains to him the procedure they are about to follow. She ends by giving the traditional assurance that:

> At the conclusion of the case, the Panel will have to consider whether the allegation is well founded. And that is all the Panel will consider at that stage. If the allegation is not well founded, then that is the end of the matter. If, however, the Panel find that the allegation is well founded, then we will move on to consider sanctions, but we only reach the sanction stage if we find the allegation against you is well founded.

This is a version of another standard statement; here is one from another case for comparison:

> The panel will retire to decide whether or not the allegation is well founded. When we return, I will read out our decision and depending on what it is, at that point we may seek further submissions in relation to sanction. That is the process we are going to follow today. Is that clear?

In today's case, the Chair repeats the phrase "case well founded" four times in four sentences. Something seems to be throwing things off balance today.

Despite the troubles emerging in the preliminary addresses, Ms Reggiori asks that the allegation be put. The HPC solicitor intervenes with two preliminary matters. First, an administrative one which concerns whether the bundles of paper in front of everyone contain the relevant pages. This is not uncommon, and simply bears witness to the administrative nightmare such formal procedures must present. Second is something called a Notice of Hearing:

> Ms Kemp: "I understand from Dr Cross's representative he wishes to make a preliminary application before the allegations are put, so I will hand over to him to make that application".

Mr Russen intervenes:

> "*Before* the allegation is put?"
>   Mr Tyme: "Yes".

Mr Russen: "Right. It would be unusual for the allegation to be put so the Panel would be able to focus on which bits of it are disputed".

There is a very brief pause while the Mr Tyme and Mr Russen whisper together, then Mr Tyme capitulates.

Mr Tyme: "You can put the allegation".

Why did Mr Tyme abandon his original plan, and so quickly? He accepts the authority of Mr Russen immediately, yet we know he had discussed this with the HPC solicitor, who had agreed that he could put his question. Why is this advice whispered? After such a show of openness, and equality, the discretion comes as quite a surprise. Nevertheless, the Hearings Officer takes her cue, and executes her responsibility:

1. "On the evening of 8 June 2009 in the course of a briefing meeting and dinner prior to a BPS accreditation visit the next day to the University of the West of England of which you were convenor:

    1. You were drunk.
    2. Because of your drunkenness you were incapable of chairing the briefing meeting.
    3. You were rude, condescending and aggressive towards a British Psychological Society employee (MR).
    4. You touched yourself inappropriately.
    5. You threatened to expose yourself.
    6. You attempted to touch OH and SP inappropriately.
    7. You made lewd suggestions to OH.

2. The matters set out in Paragraph 1(1) to (7) constitute misconduct.
3. By reason of that misconduct your fitness to practise is impaired".

The allegation has been spoken. I suppose that Mr Tyme's attempted intervention was aimed at preventing this from happening. He failed, and in failing draws our attention to the function of speech here. Having been read aloud, rather than tabled or assumed as read, it enters into the transcript of the day and becomes the property of the public no matter what the result of the case. Before this (and simultaneously), it has been written and posted on the internet, where it might be read, or indeed copied and kept by anyone in the world with a wish so to do.

The posting of the allegation surely makes the HPC responsible for getting it right at this stage. The FTP Annual Report notes a steep rise—from two percent in 2005 to thirty percent—in cases not well found this year. I duly asked the HPC's CEO to give me access to information about the process that resulted in the decision to do this in this case. He refused, saying that the work of the committee in question was confidential. I wanted to know what kind of procedures were in place to ensure that this committee did not overstep their mark—were there internal checks and balances, feedback and so on? The impossibility of finding answers to my questions (and the hostile nature of the response my questions received) prevented me from pursuing my questions at the HPC and led me to pose them here, in this book.

The allegations in this case (and in many others) pertain to non-clinical matters. They are not even academic matters. The occasion in question in Dr Cross's case is outside normal working hours. It is a private dinner, a social occasion for a few colleagues that no one is obliged to attend and that everyone is free to leave if they want to. The occasion occurred ten months prior to the hearing, and one month before the HPC and its standards applied to the registrant. Any standards being applied here—and this is still in question—are being applied in retrospect. It makes no sense as an FTP case. Does it make sense as an internal matter where the HPC wants to know more about one of its Council members? No. The government's appointments commission appoints the members of the HPC Council. Is he subject to appraisal by the administrators? No. It is the Council that is responsible for the appointment of the CEO. So what are the grounds—legal, rational, political—for this case? They are certainly not immediately apparent.

Mr Russen continues:

> Now, I wonder if I could just explain this. It is usual to ask a Registrant ... if they wish to respond to that allegation, but it is my practice to proffer some explanation before that opportunity is taken up, if it is. And it is this, that there are three distinct elements included there. And they are the three elements reflected in every HPC allegation, and they are as follows: one, the facts, and they are the facts that are alleged in the first paragraph as subparagraphs

(1) to (7) inclusive. Two, whether the facts amount to misconduct, that is to say HPC-relevant misconduct, and finally, if the facts did historically amount to misconduct, whether they are currently impairing the Registrant's fitness to practise.

He repeats the triplet that gives grounds for the HPC to act. Why—is it simply a matter of style? The style of his speech is indeed remarkable: it is overblown and pedantic.

He continues:

> Now, it can be very helpful for a Registrant to respond to the factual element of the allegation because that is something which, typically, a Registrant knows about. But a Registrant might wish to respond to the issues of misconduct and current impairment to fitness to practise. But even if there is a response to that the advice I would be giving to the Panel is [that] it is a matter for them to form their judgement about in any event.

If it is possible to summarize, he seems to say that now that the allegation has been spoken, the registrant may respond, but the panel now has the power to judge the veracity of the allegation.

> So it is now, I think, Mr Cross's opportunity to respond to the allegation which, of course, you do [through] Mr Tyme, but it is worth focusing on the fact there are those distinct elements of the facts, whether the facts were misconduct, and if there was misconduct, whether there is a current impairment of fitness to practise.

What is not questioned is the context of the action, which would render all other questions irrelevant because they are outside the jurisdiction of the HPC FTP procedures. Mr Russen, whose function it is to see that the correct law and the right procedure are followed, has missed this vital point. So what is the function of his intervention? Judging by what happens next, it might have been done in order to confuse and disorient Mr Tyme. Probably Mr Tyme knew what he wanted to say before the allegation was put, but he now seems almost incoherent. It is as if he has realized that something is supposed to be repressed but he is not exactly sure what it is.

> Mr Tyme: "I have indicated to Miss Kemp. She is aware of the proposed application. It is simply this, if I can indicate and take

you to the evidence of Owen Hughes and Sally Ross in the form of
the statements, documentation disclosed in the bundle. For present
purposes, and for present purposes only, I have to assume that the
facts are as presented for the purpose of this application only".

What does he mean? His present purpose has already been postponed
to the point of making it irrelevant. Now, he seems to be improvising
to justify his intervention ("the present purpose") but what he says is
quite opaque. I suppose, then, that he was reluctant to say what his purpose had been, having given it up so easily and having lost it forever.
As might be expected under such circumstances, what he goes on to say
hardly helps his client:

> However, if I can draw your attention to, firstly, the evidence of
> Owen Hughes, and you will find at page 3 of his statement, and if I
> can be as neutral as possible in summarising, Mr Hughes attended
> the pre-meeting on 8 June. There was some discussion, there was
> a social element, a large social element of the evening. There was a
> meal and there was drink had. And it is alleged that Mr Cross was
> inebriated, drunk.

He seems caught in a trap already laid, and sprung by the quiet word
that Mr Russen had with him. He doesn't seem to understand the way
the "law" works here and has been thrown back on his "respect" for
authority. He appears not to understand the way the HPC are using the
power they have been given. He stumbles on:

> At paragraph 3 you will see the final sentence where Mr Hughes
> said: "The format of the visit was to include a pre-accreditation
> meeting [of the BPS], a social [meeting] and, the following day, the
> formal accreditation meeting with members of the university. So in
> essence, what you have is a pre-meet, those who were attending
> the accreditation met in advance to ensure that all the participants
> were present and ready to attend the accreditation on the following
> morning."

The point he appears to be driving at is that this was a private, social
occasion and that it is not relevant to the HPC. Why does he not come
out and say this directly? He has been prevented from saying it at a
time when it would have had maximum impact, but it would still be

valuable, though it would put him at odds with the Legal Assessor and question the HPC procedures directly. This is, apparently, forbidden it is, we might say, taboo.

But there is still some way to go with Mr Tyme's intervention:

> You will see, if I may then direct you to page 24 which is, you will see it is the letter which was referred to signed by Sally Ross dated 17 September 2009. It is the third paragraph before the end and it begins "if I may". Ms Ross describes the behaviour that she complains of and goes on to say importantly: "However, whilst it is my job to attend such events, and each minute of my time spent on an accreditation visit is classed as work time, for colleagues acting as accreditation team members, it is a voluntary commitment and one which falls outside of their normal work commitments. It should also be noted that the pre-meeting was held at a time which is outside normal working hours to the volunteers. Further Dr Cross's behaviour on the day of the accreditation visit cannot be faulted and could only be described as exemplary."

Mr Tyme is clearly trying to put into question the very idea that there is any case to answer here; moreover, he is implicitly questioning the HPC's assumption that there is actually anything on which to erect a case. However, to challenge the very process that is sanctioned by law itself is like shaking your fist at God. Does this explain his reticence? We still have more than half a page of transcript to go. Perhaps it is not so surprising, now that we understand the impossible position Mr Tyme finds himself in, to discover that he goes on to shoot if not himself, then his client, in the foot:

> ... So, therefore, in my submission, with reference to the three-limb test which has quite correctly been pointed out, I query, in my submission, make submission that there is not sufficient evidence of impairment in this conduct. Misconduct maybe.

Misconduct maybe? After a full page and a half of his submission he ends up saying 'misconduct maybe'. What leads him to suggest that the case is a non-starter, and then virtually admit that his client has probably misbehaved? And what prompts this otherwise articulate young man to make so many repetitions (my submission, query, submission,

submission). My own submission is that the process is disturbed and that clarity is prevented because important information—the real reason for the case—is being suppressed. This basic interference with the path of truth appears to have forced everyone to go round the houses. This section shows Mr Tyme struggling to make his point clearly without appearing to criticize the system in which he is operating. But even now he has not finished:

> And I would invite this Panel to consider whether or not, based on the evidence as it stands, and this is the totality of the evidence before you today in relation to the specific points, of his capabilities and the manner in which he performed, whether or not that is sufficient to amount to an impairment of his fitness to practise. That is my submission.

The Chair says nothing at this point but invites Ms Kemp to reply. She uses the opportunity to repeat the HPC position—that she is confident that there is a case to be answered. However, before she restates her main points, she does concede that the Panel *could* dismiss the case at this stage if they thought that the evidence before them was not sufficient to find the registrant's fitness to practise impaired. That is, if the Panel *think* that what someone does in private is irrelevant to their business, they may throw a case out. This, however, as Mr Russen will soon say, would imply a problem with the Investigating Panel and HPC procedure. It is not clear how the HPC solicitor is implicated in this charge—is she part of the HPC or not? Has she simply picked up the brief to run with today? Or was she part of the investigatory process that built the case beforehand? This is yet another example of the ambiguity that arises as a result of the underlying belief that the HPC itself can employ no professional experts. In any case, she seems happy to go ahead with the case whether she believes in it or not. Ms Kemp continues:

> However, it is my submission that there is evidence before you which you should consider in respect of the allegation that fitness to practise is impaired. This is because impairment of fitness to practise, albeit an undefined concept in the Health Professions Council's legislation rules, has been defined or considered in the High Court in a number of cases, and it is referred to in your

Practice Note on finding of fitness to practise is impaired, which
is a Health Professions Council's practice note. It is referred to in
that Practice Note what a Panel should consider. I understand that
the Panel has these Practice Notes. The Practice Note on page 3
refers to the case of Cohen v The General Medical Council and the
reference is EWHC 581 (Admin).

Amongst the repetitions, she states that fitness to practise is an unde-
fined concept in the HPC's legislation rules, and that one must deduce
the meaning of fitness to practise from *High Court decisions* given in a
number of previous cases, usually relating to other kinds of practice.
Surely it is for the HPC to define what it means through its own intelligence and experience—the High Court judges are there for exceptional
cases. The JM report specifically pointed out that the Privy Council and
the Secretary of State had been too closely involved in the work of the
CPSM and that this should be addressed by HP0 2001. The powers of
the government, they said, should be limited to: (1) the establishment of
the initial Council; (2) the appointment of specific members of Council;
(3) approval of minor matters (rules and procedures); (4) approval of
new professions to the Register; and (5) to act as a final court of appeal
when appropriate. By pulling in High Court decisions as reference
points for this particular Panel, Ms Kemp short-circuits the system and
seems to show her own ambitions and preferred reference points. She
puts the wisdom of the hearing completely outside the domain not only
of the experts in question and of the HPC partners but into the hands
of High Court judges. It might be worth noting here that mechanisms
which collect and support any wisdom generated by the experience of
its Panels seem to be lacking at the HPC. This is hardly likely to ensure
that real justice will be done.

The practice note (which can be downloaded from the HPC website:
http://www.hpc-uk.org/publications/practicenotes/) refers explicitly
to the case of the General Medical Council v Meadow and to the High
Court appeal made in Cohen v GMC. The case of Sir Roy Meadow refers
to the evidence he gave in the case of Sally Clark, which led to her being
convicted of murdering her two children. She was later cleared on both
counts when the deaths were declared "cot deaths". It is difficult to see
what relevance this has to today's case. However, there is one factor that
does provide a link from the GMC case to the HPC. The Chair of the

GMC panel that struck off Sir Roy Meadow was Mary Clark Glass, who is a lay member of HPC Council and a lay member of the GMC. She is (somewhat ironically) reported as having told Sir Roy: "You should not have strayed into areas that were not within your remit of expertise". In order to understand the ruling, it seems necessary to deduce that he was struck off for having too much influence over the jury. This completely ignores the process of law, and the role of all the others involved in the case. It would seem more appropriate to have taken him off the expert witness list if it were felt he was using his charisma to hypnotize the court, or to recruit court members less susceptible to charm and more interested in facts. Finally, the case of Roy Meadow is on a whole different level from the one we are concerned with here—there are matters of life and death at stake in one which are totally absent in the other. Yet it is the reference point in today's hearing at the HPC.

The second case is also drawn from the medical world. The Panel had found that the fitness to practice of Cohen (an anaesthetist) was impaired and had imposed conditions upon his registration. He appealed to the High Court, which essentially agreed with the Panel that mistakes had been made but disagreed with the level of sanction.

The HPC Practice Note draws the following interesting lessons from this case (Cohen v GMC):

> The initial task for the Panel is: *"To consider the [allegations] and decide on the evidence whether the [allegations] are proved in a way in which a jury ... has to decide whether the defendant is guilty of each count in the indictment. At this stage, the Panel is not considering any other aspect of the case, such as whether the [Registrant] has a good record or ... performed any other aspect of the case, performed any other aspect of the work ... with the required level of skill".* Subsequently, the Panel is: *"concerned with the issue of whether in the light of any misconduct [etc] proved, the fitness of the [Registrant] to practise has been impaired taking account of the critically important public policy issues".*

Those "critically important public policy issues" which must be taken into account by Panels were described by the court as:

> *the need to protect the individual patient and the collective need to maintain confidence in the profession as well as declaring and upholding proper*

standards of conduct and behaviour which the public expect ... and that
public interest includes amongst other things the protection of patients
and maintenance of public confidence in the profession.

This case is concerned with the "the care of a patient (B) who had
been due to undergo major surgery. Although C administered the
anaesthetic without fault, it was alleged that his pre-operative and post-
operative care and assessment and his note-taking and note-keeping
fell significantly below the required standard". Without knowing any
of the details of the pre- and post-operative care, it seems likely that the
physical well-being of a patient was intimately involved in this case.
It is very unclear what parallels there are with Dr Cross's case. It is,
however, perfectly clear that there are none that pertain to Dr Cross as
a registrant.

Ms Kemp goes on to give her synopsis of that case (and no one shouts
"objection"—indeed, to whom would they object?):

> The High Court in Cohen said that the Panel is concerned with the
> issues of whether in the light of any misconduct proved the fitness
> of the health professional to practise had been impaired taking
> account of the critically important public policy issues. It goes on to
> say that those public policy issues are, the need to protect the indi-
> vidual patient and the collective need to maintain confidence in the
> profession, as well as declaring and upholding proper standards of
> conduct and behaviour which the public expect, and that the pub-
> lic interest includes, among other things, the protection of patients
> and maintenance of public confidence in the profession.

It is interesting that she keeps her reference to the generalized rule in
order to transfer the influence from the GMC, and it is perhaps more
interesting that no one here calls her on it. She goes on:

> Those public policy issues and those considerations can take two
> forms. They can take the form of a consideration of a Registrant's
> capability in terms of their ability to practise. But also their suit-
> ability to practise. And suitability takes into account personal
> conduct. And this is a case that involves such conduct, and one of
> the aspects which Registrants of the HPC are required to consider
> which is set out in the Standards of Conduct, Performance and

Ethics at Paragraph 3 is that Registrants must keep high standards of personal conduct. It says "You must keep high standards of personal conduct, as well as professional conduct. You should be aware that poor conduct outside your professional life may still affect someone's confidence in you and your profession".

So whilst it is accepted that this incident involving Dr Cross occurred in, effectively, three stages. There was a pre-meeting in respect of the accreditation visit. Then, secondly, a social event. And then, thirdly, there was the accreditation visit itself. You can look at conduct which occurred in the social aspect of this case, but also in the pre-meeting which was in work context. So those aspects of conduct can be considered. In my submission, there is evidence which goes to personal conduct which falls to be considered and it would be better dealt with by the Panel in my submission if it were to hear the evidence before you today. So the evidence of Mr Hughes and Sally Ross, and [you will] also hear from Dr Cross and then come to your own determination whether you consider fitness to practise impaired.

The registrant's representative is given another chance to respond, but declines. He lets the case of the anaesthetist go unchallenged as a reference point. This leaves it open to Mr Russen, who takes a deep breath and launches into another long intervention:

Well, I think the Panel has to be very clear about what it is being asked to do. And it is not being asked to form a judgment as to whether or not Dr Cross's current fitness to practice is impaired.

Before continuing with Mr Russen's argument, let us look once again at the phrase "fitness to practice" which appears here. We have heard nothing whatsoever about the registrant's practice as a counselling psychologist. We have heard that his competency at chairing a BPS accreditation visit to a university was exemplary. We might begin to wonder at the scope of the power the HPC assumes it possesses. Not only does it easily assume an interest in the registrant's work at the university, but also in his private affairs. This is justified through a standard which asks its registrants not to bring the profession into disrepute. But which profession? It is not the profession of counselling psychologists, nor of psychologists, nor even of scholars. The only thing that makes sense, albeit very little, is to assume he is being judged as a Health Professions *Councillor*.

At this stage of the proceedings it seems very likely that the case of Dr Cross is being held to prove that the HPC itself is innocent of any misdemeanour. This is a double fudge of the way things are supposed to proceed. First, although Dr Cross is in the dock, it is the HPC that is on trial. Second, the misdemeanour does not represent any harm to the public, but constitutes a danger to the self-image of the HPC. It is possible to begin sketching a hypothesis about this case—it is being conducted in order to prove to some vague observer, a "big other", that the HPC is without stain.

Mr Russen is giving advice to the Panel before they retire to consider Mr Tyme's rather unclear request. They seem to know what he is asking. Had he spoken before the allegations, he might have been asking them to abandon the hearing for lack of any real evidence of any particular offence. Speaking after the allegation, he has been put into a different position, one that Mr Russen goes on to demolish. He reminds the Panel that they are not, in fact, being asked to form a judgement as to whether or not Dr Cross's current fitness to practise is impaired. No, he continues:

> ... that is emphatically not what the Panel should be doing. What the Panel is being asked to do is to look at this evidence on paper without having heard any witnesses the HPC intends to call, and to say whether what is written on paper, the behaviour that is recorded on paper, could amount to a current impairment of fitness to practise.

There should be an emphasis placed on the word "could" and that is clearly the question that the Investigating Committee is responsible for answering.

> It would be quite inappropriate to do that in the circumstances where you have not heard the evidence.

Mr Russen begins from a different point from Mr Tyme. He takes for granted the rightness of the Investigatory Panel's decision, and refuses to allow it to be questioned. What will happen if the case is eventually to be found "unproven"? Will that reopen the question about the quality of HPC's investigatory process? We are not to know—the CEO sidestepped these questions, posed to him in a letter after the case.

> What you are being invited to do is to say that, in effect, even if the HPC's case is proved to the hilt as we understand it to be capable of proof from the documents, even if that happens it will not be possible for a Panel doing its job properly to take the view that this was behaviour that could amount to current impairment of fitness to practise.

Not only is he refusing to allow a question to be posed about whether this case should have come forward to public hearing, but he then uses, as an example, the possibility that the HPC case is proved, whereas Mr Tyme is arguing that it is untenable. He affirms confidence in the Investigatory Committee's process to put forward a case worth considering: *"even if the HPC's case is proved to the hilt as we understand it to be capable of proof from the documents"*. He appears to be spinning Mr Tyme's question.

> "And it is worth noting", he goes on, that the focus of this submission is on the last element of the consideration that a Panel has to undertake in order to say an allegation is well founded or not it carries with it the necessary implication that misconduct, for the purposes of this application, that misconduct is established. That has to be the case because you would not be considering impairment of fitness to practise if there was no misconduct.

Mr Russen thus reminds the panel yet again that there is a process they must follow, and that this requires them to first split the thing up into three elements, and then to organize those elements in sequence. It reminds me of the techniques that professors of computer science once used to get people to begin to think about writing a computer programme—write down step by step what you must do to make a cup of tea. Each attempt to write it down always failed because of some minute detail that had been overlooked. (Did you take the lid off the kettle before you filled it up? Did you place it under the cold water tap to get the water in? Did you "fill it up", which would over-ride the circuitry, or did you "fill it up" to just above the element, etc., ad infinitum.) The end result is to make you think you don't have the slightest idea how to make a cup of tea. So here the Panel is told that it cannot do what common sense might tell it to do, but must follow the procedure laid down in the rule book. Of course, process is important, but it is this that Mr Tyme is questioning. Mr Russen's intervention manages to make it look as if Mr Tyme is the one who needs reminding of the importance of procedure! There is a strange distortion occurring which rejects both the value and the logic of Mr Tyme's question.

> Now, I think the Panel have to be careful about this. Reference has been made by Mr Tyme to the evidence that the following day at the validation meeting properly Dr Cross behaved impeccably and did his professional job properly, there is no suggestion that I have seen in the papers anywhere that that is going to be gainsaid by the evidence the HPC might expect to call.

So at no point will it be said that Dr Cross has been incompetent in his job as an academic course accreditor. He goes on:

> But it is not what this allegation brought by the HPC against Dr Cross is about because if you look at the allegation on page 6 of the letter, it is confined to the pre-meeting and dinner the previous day.

Here Mr Russen is using a different logic from Ms Kemp. She uses the third meeting to define the first two; he separates the third completely from the first two. It appears a sleight of hand. The plot thickens:

> So I think the HPC are going to have to argue, because you have not heard an opening from Ms Kemp yet, but the HPC are going to have to confine whatever case they construct against Dr Cross on the basis of those facts. So they are going to say those facts amount to misconduct, and that is to say misconduct which is properly to be considered by the HPC, and that that past misconduct is currently impairing Dr Cross's fitness to practise.

We already know that, in the ordinary use of language, Dr Cross's past conduct, good or bad, private or public, has not impaired his fitness to *practise* anything at all (other than, of course; charm in the presence of his enemies). That is, his fitness *to do the job* he is engaged to do, which, in this case, is an academic accreditation, and not his work as a counselling psychologist. Nor has he frightened any member of the public into thinking the whole profession either of psychologists or of health professionals are dangerous scoundrels. I am not at all clear which part of Mr Russen's job he is, or is not, doing at the moment.

To recap, he had been very clear at the beginning: "I am a lawyer and my primary job is to ensure that these proceedings are conducted properly in the sense that the correct procedure is followed and the right law applied". Mr Russen has interpreted his role as safeguarding the work of the Investigatory Committee, ensuring that its decision to put this case in the public domain is upheld, no matter that there is only evidence that the registrant is excellent at his job, no matter that this job is the business of academic accreditation. It is not possible to discern any law that is at stake here—no legal expertise is needed.

Where is the judge who might call for order? Where is the lawyer who might extend an objection. Who is empowered to impose common sense? It is the Panel who must take or reject Mr Russen's advice. They are too polite, I suppose, to ask him to shut up. Mr Russen knows that he is speaking outside his formal remit, however, and is about to say as much himself:

> Again, it is not for me to say what the HPC's case is and is not, but I would venture to suggest from the papers we have been served it is not going to be the HPC's case that this behaviour demonstrates a propensity on the part of Dr Cross to get drunk and behave outrageously.

If this is not the HPC's case, then what is it?

> There is no hint of that anywhere, and I do not imagine it is going to be suggested to you, and if it is I would suggest that it should not be suggested to you, that Dr Cross presents a risk to patients or clients, both present and prospective, that he is going to turn up for sessions with them blotto and behave inappropriately towards them.

It is not going to be suggested to you, and if it is going to be suggested to you I would suggest that it should not be suggested to you—what explains this verbal excess? What position is Mr Russen speaking from? He seems to have taken over the role of Ms Kemp. So much for what is not going to happen. He now turns to what he imagines will happen:

What the HPC are, if I understand the matters correctly, suggesting is that to behave on an occasion which could not be said to be wholly social because of the reason that everybody was there, this behaviour was behaviour of a sort that is of legitimate concern to the HPC and is of legitimate concern to the HPC because it would be behaviour which, perhaps absent some explanation, would cause patients/clients to have concerns about Dr Cross as a professional. And that would seem to be the basis from the papers on which the HPC might be able to say that there is current impairment of fitness to practise. Namely, a public confidence in the profession.

Just what is going on here? Why is Mr Russen repeating and restating the HPC case? He has supported the HPC position that this occasion constitutes one worth its attention, because there might be a section of the public who, if they saw or heard about this, would lose confidence in Dr Cross. This seems bizarre. There is more:

So, to come back to the submission you are being asked to rule upon, in effect, you are being asked to say that the evidence of the information that you have is such that a Panel doing its job properly could not come to the conclusion, note could not, not should not, should not might be a further question, but could not is the one that will have to be relevant for present purposes. That conduct as appearing on the face of the papers is behaviour that could not result in a finding of current impairment of fitness to practise on the basis I have sought to articulate. That is a judgment for the Panel. I do not think it is appropriate for me to say any more than that. That, I think, is the consideration the Panel should be giving to it.

But after just a brief moment where the HPC lawyer declines the offer to say more, and Mr Tyme nods his head, which Mr Russen takes as a sign of agreement (at least to his authority and direction, if not to the logic of his statement), he continues:

I would venture to suggest one more thing, and it is this, clearly if the Panel finds favour in the submission Mr Tyme has made then you should come back and I think it would be appropriate, if, indeed, I think the Panel specifically should give reasons for acceding to it because particularly as this is an allegation that has been through the HPC Investigatory Committee where that Committee has found that there is a case to answer. I think this Panel should explain why it accedes to the allegation.

The Panel is set up properly before it goes off to think about its decision, and is finally reminded that its colleagues would be called into question if they responded in favour of Mr Tyme's petition. But it is not over yet:

> If on the other hand the Panel does not accede to the application that has been made, I think the Panel should simply say that it does not accede to the application that has been made on behalf of Dr Cross, and the reason for that is at some point the Panel is going to have to form, it if does not accede to it, a decision on the very issue that is the subject matter of this application, and it is undesirable in those circumstances for the Panel to say why it does not accede to it in circumstances where it is then going to have to make what I can probably call the balanced judgement.

Mr Russen introduced himself as someone who advises on law but does not involve himself in the decision of the Panel. Here, however, he seems to be putting words into their mouths, or attempting to. Let's see what the Panel make of it. They retire to discuss their decision, saying: "If we need any further advice, we will call upon the Legal Assessor". What law is being invoked here? It is difficult to see one. Mr Tyme seems confused about whether or not it is wrong for someone to perhaps be drunk amongst colleagues at a social event, but he does seem to want to say that probably it is not sufficient to warrant a hearing. Mr Russen has taken pains to explain the minutiae of HPC procedure in breaking things down and distributing them, including the responsibility the Panel has today in respecting the Investigating Committee's decision. Ms Kemp reminds them they are also subject to the authority of the High Court judges. The Panel knows it needs to discuss this, and takes advantage of the facilities the HPC offers it to do so in private. There is a room set aside for the Panel: glass walls, of course, so they can be seen to be working, but where their words will not be recorded. They adjourn for about half an hour.

They stand up together, turn together, and leave the room together. The four of us in the audience, two members of the public and two reporters, relax and look at each other as if to ask what on earth is going on. At which point the Hearings Officer comes to ask us to leave the room and go back to wait in reception. This takes me by surprise—I have never yet been asked to leave the room when the Panel retires. I was a little alarmed to see the two journalists pick up their things and leave in a hurry. I didn't know what they knew, or how they knew it, so I asked Ms Dwomoh-Bonsu why we were being asked to leave. Now it was she who was taken by surprise. She gave a rather incoherent reply, grasping for some kind of logic to answer my question. We had a little to and fro where I asked for the rationale, and she tried to supply one, until we established that she didn't really know whose rule this was, nor why it was being invoked on this occasion. While we were thus engaged, Mr Russen suddenly reappeared and demanded of me: "Are you refusing to leave the room?" This was alarming. He had positioned himself in a very imposing stance. I broke my attention from Ms Dwomoh-Bonsu—we were in mid-sentence, but his question demanded immediate and prior attention—and said: "No, I am trying to understand why I am being asked". He turned on his heels and left the room, leaving us to carry on our rather stilted conversation. This didn't last much longer, as she could only say that the room was needed for the private conversations of the lawyers, and to turn and gesture to the empty chairs where the lawyers were no longer sitting. To which I responded: "But there is nobody here, and this has never been asked of me before". Soon she left us, and my colleague and I found ourselves alone in the large and airy room, wondering what this power struggle had been about, and why we were feeling so bruised as a consequence. Ms Dwomoh-Bonsu then reappeared with another young woman, who told us quite clearly that we must leave the room in order to let the lawyers have a private conversation. Again this order was accompanied by a gesture towards the large and empty room. This time, however, I said: "I will obey you, but I don't understand why you are taking such pains". We got up and crossed the threshold of the room behind the Manager. As soon as her mission had been accomplished, she turned to some other business and left us stranded. She had simply wanted us to obey her instruction—it was a simple demonstration of power. And now the Panel and the other players were returning to their seats and we followed them straight back into the room. This point is neither trivial nor personal. It simply shows that various agents of the HPC are prone to use the institutional power for no particular purpose or reason other than the exercise of that power.

The Panel took up their seats, and the atmosphere of the room returned to that of a hearing in progress. The Panel Chair drew breath and looked straight at Dr Cross, ready to deliver the decision. But Mr Russen intervened:

> I appreciate that the Panel has a decision on the application, but there is a matter I think I should mention first, and it is a matter that the Panel will be unaware of, and it is this, that as the Panel are probably aware, when the Panel leaves this room to have private deliberations, it is the norm for members of the public and the press to leave this room.

In my admittedly limited experience of some dozen hearings, not only have I never been asked to leave the room when the Panel leaves the room, but I've also been able to ask questions of others remaining in the room, who always (including Mr Russen on occasion) politely tried to answer me. I even once asked Mr Russen if it was okay to be in the room, to which he had said yes.

> One of the reasons for that is so there is the opportunity for those who need to have confidential discussions about the case to be able to do that without the risk of being overheard.

The HPC makes available small private rooms for the registrant and his supporters, and another small private room for the Panel. No such provision is made for the lawyers.

> "There are two people", he continued, looking directly at me and my colleague "there are two people present, I do not know if they are members of the press, or members of the public. There"—and everyone in the room turned and fixed me in their gaze—"There is the lady in the black jacket".

I looked down at my jacket and fished the yellow tag out from the folds and held it up for all to clearly see and said

> My name is Janet Low, I'm a member of the public.

The Legal Assessor thanked me, and added

> And the gentleman sitting next to her.
> Bruce Scott
> Thank you. Who were not prepared to leave at that point. I think it is right that the Panel should be aware of that, because it does potentially affect the ability that the parties have to make discussions about things.

How can one explain this? Has Mr Russen invested himself too much in the process, has he mistaken his role and overstepped the boundaries of his work? It seems so. But one still needs to ask, why? This is a man who spends a great deal of time at the HPC as Legal Assessor—he has plenty of experience here. He is sub-contracted as an independent expert. Why has this case rattled him? On the one hand you might say that a newly appointed Council member going through the process would give plenty of cause for anxiety, but why? If the system works, and he implies that it does, then the decision of the Investigating Committee to put Dr Cross's case forward for hearing should sop up the excess anxiety. Perhaps there is an added twist here that gives rise to the problem. This could be an attempt on the part of the HPC to have it both ways: to prove themselves capable of putting their own professionals through the process, to show themselves to be just and fair, but with the expectation that they would be able to turn the process in such a way as to exonerate the accused and leave everything in place. It is possible.

He goes on:

> Of course the Panel does have a residual power. I am not suggesting that they should wield it now but the Panel does have a power to exclude people from the proceedings.

Why would Mr Russen want to exclude people from these proceedings? One answer would be that this case represents a significant threat to the HPC, and that he is sufficiently identified with the HPC to want to guard it from that threat. But what is the threat? And how is it associated with whether or not I leave an empty room that I have been permitted to stay in on previous occasions? Even though the situation was resolved when I simply obeyed the order, it seems unlikely that this alone was a sufficient signifier of danger.

But I think the Panel should be aware of the fact that whereas other people, the two gentlemen who I think may be members of the press, certainly one is a member of the press sitting beyond the two I have identified were prepared to move. Those two were not. It may be that we will have to return to that issue at some point. Sorry, I probably disrupted your announcement.

The immediate effect of all this was to put my name and that of my colleague into the record, to put everyone's eyes on us, to let us feel the weight of his power and to identify the journalists who were present. Presumably this was done to avert a danger—but what danger? Mr Russen said that people must leave the room in order not to over-hear private conversations that might have taken place. Is there a secret between the lawyers? It is all nonsense. Kafkaesque.

Nevertheless the Panel Chair lets Mr Russen speak, but when he is finished, she dismisses his words completely by returning her gaze to Dr Cross and delivers the Panel's decision:

> The Panel have considered the representations made by Mr Tyme and Ms Kemp and the Panel are not prepared to accede to the appli-cation from Mr Tyme. In view of that, [are] there any further repre-sentations you wish to make about the allegation at this stage?
>   Mr Tyme: "No".

So the registrant's lawyer is defeated by HPC procedure. But there is one more consideration to be addressed before the hearing can begin.

Chair: "Ms Kemp, before you open on behalf of the Health Profes-sions Council there are two matters that the Panel would like to raise with you, one of the exhibits is a letter from your witness, Ms Ross, to Ms Johnson, the Director of Fit-ness to Practise".

Ms Kemp: "Yes".

Chair: "That appears to be in response to a letter from Ms Johnson dated 28 August 2009; are you going to give us copies of that letter so we can see—"

Ms Kemp: —"The letter of Ms Johnson, I was not proposing to do so. However, if there are no objections from Mr Tyme, there is no issue that turns on it, but if the Panel feel it would be

> assisted and there are no objections, I do not see why you should not have a copy of it".
>
> Chair: "Mr Tyme".
>
> Mr Tyme: "No objection".
>
> Ms Kemp: "No objection".
>
> Chair: "I think it would be helpful because we only really have one half of the picture".
>
> Ms Kemp: "Yes, madam. I have one copy here. I could ask Ms Dwomoh-Bonsu to copy the letter, make copies available for the Panel and Legal Assessor".

This perhaps means that the Panel, whilst in private deliberation, spent some of the time going through the paperwork together, and noticed some anomalies. I wonder what the usual routine is for a Panel. A hearing typically starts at 10 a.m., but perhaps it is customary for the Panel to meet at 9 a.m. to go through the case together. In any case, whether they talked just before the hearing or not, they missed the fact that this letter was missing, or missed the fact that it mattered. From our point of view, however, it introduces us to Ms Johnson and begins to raise a question. Who is she, what role does she play, and what qualifies her in this position? In fact she is the "Director" of Fitness to Practise. This deserves a note—the "Director" of FTP is a rather misleading title. Kelly Johnson is not an experienced practitioner, nor, in the normal use of the word a "senior" member of staff. She is in fact a rather young woman whose qualifications are more to do with liaison and efficiency than experience and judgement (her job description can be found at http://hpcwatchdog.blogspot.com/2011/06/job-description-head-of-case-management.html).

There is yet one more administrative detail to be covered before the Chair is ready to begin.

> Chair: "The other matter is, obviously it is a matter for you which witness you call, there is no statement from the witness, from the person whose initials are SP".
>
> Ms Kemp: "That is right, madam, not as part of the Health Professions Council's case".
>
> Chair: "Thank you".
>
> Mr Tyme: "Madam, it may help if I can indicate he has provided, if I assume it is the person who, the present—"

Ms Kemp: "—Yes".

Mr Tyme: "He has in fact provided character evidence on behalf of the Registrant. I do have a statement which I can hand up to the Panel at the appropriate time".

Chair: "That is fine. Thank you very much. Ms Kemp".

With these administrative details sorted, and now that the kind of calm that only administrative details can invoke has been re-established, Ms Reggiori invites Ms Kemp to open the proceedings.

CHAPTER THREE

FTP detail

Ms Kemp: "... You are considering an allegation in accordance with article 27(3)I of the HPO2001. You are considering an allegation made against Dr Cross which has been made under article 22(1)(a)i. That allegation, as you have heard, which was read out to you by the Hearings Officer, is that Dr Cross's fitness to practise is impaired by reason of misconduct. And the overarching allegation is based upon particulars 1(7) of the Notice of Allegation dated 10 November 2009. That appears at page 6. You have heard already this morning from your Learned Assessor and also Mr Tyme that you consider the allegation in three stages. Firstly, is the factual element well founded, that is, proved on the balance of probabilities, and the Health Professions Council bears the burden of proof. Secondly, you then go on to consider whether those facts, if you find them to be proved, amount to misconduct. That is a matter for your professional judgement. Thirdly, if you do find that those facts amount to misconduct you consider whether fitness to practise is impaired as a result of today's date".

I propose to open this case following those distinct stages. So, firstly, I propose to outline the factual elements of the case. And you will hear from two witnesses in this case. The first is Owen Hughes, who is a consultant counselling psychologist. He was attending an accreditation visit to the University of West of England on 8 and 9 June 2009 together with Dr Cross, Molly Ross, and also Simon Parritt who was responsible for assisting Dr Cross. As I said, the second witness is Molly Ross, who was the BPS representative.

You have heard already from Mr Tyme that the visit on the 8 and 9 June was for the purpose of accrediting the university's counselling psychology doctorate course. And Dr Cross was responsible for convening this accreditation visit. In my submission it is helpful for the Panel to consider this accreditation visit in three stages, or put it another way consisted of three elements. First of all, there was the pre-visit meeting, which took place on the evening of the 8 June 2009 in the early part of the evening. Secondly, the second element was a social element. It is accepted that it was a social element which was an evening meal which took place immediately after the meeting on 8 June 2009 and was attended by all those who had attended the pre-visit meeting. And then the third element was the accreditation visit itself which took place at the university on 9 June 2009.

The allegation that you are considering only concerns the first two elements of the visit, so the pre-meeting and the social element.

First, the repetition of the word "allegation" (six times in the first eleven lines). Second, the repetition of the three-part process that is to be followed. Third, the repetition of the device which splits the occasion into three parts in order to justify the HPC interest in it.

And it is right to say that during the accreditation visit itself the conduct of Dr Cross is not in question at all. Molly Ross in her letter to Kelly Johnson which appears at Exhibit MR/1 at page 24 it is clear from Ms Ross's letter that she thought his behaviour on the day of the accreditation visit cannot be faulted and can only be described as exemplary. So very much confined to those first two elements of the visit.

So turning then to the conduct that concerns you and the first element of the visit: the pre-visit meeting. The first three sub-paragraphs, so paragraphs (1) to (3) of the allegation relate to this pre-meeting visit. You will hear from Owen Hughes that the meeting was to commence at 6.30 p.m. but Dr Cross did not arrive until 6.45 p.m. Mr Hughes states in his witness statement that at this time, he (Dr Cross) was clearly very drunk, he was slurring his words, speaking loudly and was very unsteady on his feet.

Molly Ross in her letter to Kelly Johnson confirms this and states that Dr Cross was incapable of chairing the pre-meeting. That appears at Exhibit MR/1, page 22. She also states that Dr Cross commented that, 'I was a different person, and that I was grumpy and whispered loudly to other team members that he wished another of my colleagues was there because I was more fun [sic]. He also queried what exactly are you here for?' It is that conduct which relates to sub-particular (3) of the allegation.

"Sub-particular 3 states: you were rude, condescending, and aggressive towards a BPS employee (MR)". As members of the audience we don't have access to the written documents that make up so much of this hearing. We must rely on the solicitors to bring out that which is necessary from the text and put it into words. It is not clear here who is being unclear—is it Molly Ross's letter that is unclear, or Ms Kemp's rendition of it that is unclear?

The second phase of the visit was the social element. This was a visit to a restaurant in Bristol. All those present at the meeting, together with Mr Parritt's wife, went to the restaurant. Owen Hughes says that Dr Cross continued to drink constantly throughout the meal. There appears, in my submission, to have been two stages to this meal, the first element was that early on, according to Mr Hughes, there appeared to have been sensible conversations, as he describes it, with Dr Cross. The second stage appears to be later on in the evening, and Owen Hughes states as both the night and his drunkenness progressed Dr Cross became more sexually inappropriate. And so it is at this later stage in the evening that the conduct alleged in sub-particulars (4) to (7) took place. And the evidence of those is set out by Mr Hughes in his statement and Paragraph 12 on page 13 of his statement Mr Hughes says that "he", again meaning Dr Cross, "began by rubbing Simon Parritt's upper thigh while putting his arm around him. Simon Parritt's wife was with him at the dinner and did not look comfortable. Simon Parritt appeared to laugh it off. I should say I have paraphrased some of that statement. Hopefully, I will be corrected if I have paraphrased it to a greater degree than is warranted".

Paraphrasing would have been welcome!

> The next element of conduct which caused Mr Hughes concern is
> set out at Paragraph 13 at page 13. Mr Hughes describes that "he",
> meaning Dr Cross, started to tell me that he loved me and asked me
> repeatedly to kiss him and leaned over the table in an attempt to
> kiss me. In the same paragraph Mr Hughes says that Dr Cross then
> offered Mr Hughes oral sex before leaning back in his chair and
> rubbing his crotch. So that is the evidence from Mr Hughes which
> relates to those sub-particulars (4) to (7). Those are the factual ele-
> ments of the allegation.

It is quite difficult to understand what Ms Kemp means by "factual"
here. Everything is reported and only by two of the people who are
directly concerned, and nothing has been put the test. These words
support the four final points of the allegation: (4) that you touched
yourself inappropriately, (5) you threatened to expose yourself, (6) you
attempted to touch OH and SP inappropriately, and (7) you made lewd
suggestions to OH. The third point we have just seen relates to his being
rude, condescending and aggressive to Molly Ross. The first two points
being (1) you were drunk, and (2) because of your drunkenness you
were incapable of chairing the briefing meeting.

> The next matter for you to consider is misconduct, and it is the
> Council's case that straightforwardly Dr Cross's conduct was
> inappropriate and fell below the professional standards required
> of Registrants and, therefore, it amounts to misconduct and you
> would consider of course in this respect the standards of con-
> duct, performance and ethics. I have already referred you to Para-
> graph 3.

The Council here makes the case that Dr Cross's behaviour fell below
its standards without making an argument to support the statement; it
is simply asserted and then given the status of misconduct. No rationale is offered to as to why the allegations are held to constitute a danger to the public, no argument is made as to how offensive behaviour
constitutes a problem to the profession. It is reasonable to expect the
HPC to be able to articulate its reasons for making this an offence for
which a person might lose his right to work, especially given the action
(which we shall come to later) of the BPS itself in the matter.

Next comes the question of whether this behaviour constitutes a danger to Dr Cross's patients—is he fit to practise as a counselling psychologist? Again, no arguments at all are constructed to lead from this event to any work that might be considered clinical. And none are made to demonstrate how this evening's shenanigans constitute a danger to the newly forming Health Profession itself. It might be more true to say that Mr Hughes had lost confidence in Dr Cross as a gentleman and it is this that provides the grounds to argue that a danger is present. Yet none of this is said. Why not? From what follows we can see that the lawyer avoids reasoning her case and relies on repeating the three-part list in order to proceed.

> Moving on then, finally, to the question of impairment of fitness to practise. This is a question entirely for the Panel. And it is a question that you will have to consider carefully, and you will have to consider carefully whether the misconduct, if you find it to be misconduct, on 8 June 2009 impairs Dr Cross's fitness to practise as of today's date because of course you look forward and not back.

She is going out of her way to instruct the panel on its duties and obligations, which one might have hoped was something they already understood, given their place in this drama.

> It is a matter of judgment for the Panel, and, in my submission you will have to take into account three factors. Firstly, the incident of 8 June 2009 and the circumstances surrounding it as you have found them to be. Secondly, Dr Cross's insight. And, thirdly, guidance issued by the High Court and Court of Appeal which is set out in your Practice Note.

Let us review the legal framework for this allegation. Ms Kemp introduced this when she mentioned Article 27(3)i of the Health Professions Order 2001. HPO 2001 is a piece of secondary legislation set up using powers laid down in section 62(9) of the Health Act 1999 (the primary legislation brought in by the Labour Government as a major part of its work for "modernising" the health service). Article 27 is in Part V (entitled "Fitness to Practise of the HPO 2001") and is headed "The Conduct and Competence Committee". Here is the detail of that article as it appeared in the original publication (2002):

Article 27
The Conduct and Competence Committee shall—

a. having consulted the other Practice Committees as it thinks appropriate, advise the Council (whether on the Council's request or otherwise) on—
    i. the performance of the Council's functions in relation to standards of conduct, performance and ethics expected of registrants and prospective registrants,
    ii. requirements as to good character and good health to be met by registrants and prospective registrants, and
    iii. the protection of the public from people whose fitness to practise is impaired; and
b. consider—
    i. any allegation referred to it by the Council, Screeners, the Investigating Committee or the Health Committee, and
    ii. any application for restoration referred to it by the Registrar.

And here is the same section as it appears in the new and amended version of the order, published in 2009;

The Conduct and Competence Committee

Article 27
The Conduct and Competence Committee shall—

a. ...
b. consider—
    i. any allegation referred to it by the Council, Screeners, the Investigating Committee or the Health Committee, and
    ii. any application for restoration referred to it by the Registrar.

The Health Committee

Article 28
The Health Committee shall consider—

There doesn't appear to be a paragraph 3 subsection (i) in either version. Perhaps there was a small error either in Ms Kemp's speech, or in the transcript. Or maybe she was wrong and no one noticed. She went on to say "You are considering an allegation made against Dr Cross which has been made under article 22(1)(a)i." This paragraph comes within the same Part V of HPO 2001 and bears the heading:

Allegations

22. 1. This article applies where any allegation is made against a registrant to the effect that—

a. his fitness to practise is impaired by reason of—
   i. misconduct,
   ii. lack of competence,
   iii. a conviction or caution in the United Kingdom for a criminal offence, or a conviction elsewhere for an offence which, if committed in England and Wales, would constitute a criminal offence,
   iv. his physical or mental health, or
   v. a determination by a body in the United Kingdom responsible under any enactment for the regulation of a health or social care profession to the effect that his fitness to practise is impaired, or a determination by a licensing body elsewhere to the same effect;

This is the reference point that allows the HPC to move forward with proceedings if it believes that misconduct has taken place. In the latest version of the order (July 2009) misconduct, however, is not defined.

The legal framework that surrounds and grounds the HPC is important to trace and discuss. We have seen that the JM report remarked that fitness to practise proceedings should expand to consider more than just "infamous behaviour".

There are also the normal rhetorical devices one might expect from a lawyer: Mrs Parritt, for example, is stated clearly as *being* uncomfortable, but her husband only *appeared* to laugh it off. One is definite, the other is conditional. Dr Cross *is clearly* drunk, but only *appears to be* conducting a sensible conversation. These are all little tricks, and no one is objecting. Perhaps we can assume that the Panel notes these and discounts them. Perhaps.

The HPC calls its first witness, Mr Owen Hughes, who is sworn in. Ms Kemp begins her questions:

> Ms Kemp: I am going to start by asking the questions and,
>   although I ask the questions, you should direct your
>   answers to the Panel, because they are the people who
>   will be considering your evidence.

This is frequently said in hearings at the HPC. It is a straightforward admission that the room has been laid out without proper consideration to its function. The room contains foldaway tables and chairs on wheels. Why has someone not given a bit of thought to the practicalities of design? The assumption that can be read behind the layout is that layout has no role in the process, no role in the realm of meaning, no realm in human interaction.

Ms Kemp proceeds to establish that Mr Hughes is who is says he is—a counselling psychologist of ten years standing, and that it is indeed he and not another. As she does this there is another one of those tedious hiccups that regularly occur as she asks him to confirm his signature, but the bundle in front of him does not contain that particular document either on page 10 or page 14.

> Ms Kemp: Maybe Mr Hughes has a different bundle [Legal As-
>   sessor handed bundle]. If it assists, madam, in the
>   preparation of the bundles there is always a prelimi-
>   nary copy which is sent out to the HPC FTP Depart-
>   ment to check and sometimes the witness statement is
>   sent approved, but unsigned, and then at a later stage a
>   signed copy is sent through. Therefore, there has been
>   a mix up in the bundle which appeared on the witness
>   stand.
> Miss Reggiori: Certainly in my bundle I have a signed copy.

They sort it out and the process continues, with Ms Kemp asking permission to ask questions supplementary to the statements. Miss Reggiori grants permission and Ms Kemp first establishes the long-term nature of the relationship between Mr Hughes and Dr Cross:

> Ms Kemp: If I can ask you to turn to page 10 of your statement, at
>   Paragraph 2, approximately half way down the para-
>   graph, it is the second to last sentence you say: "For
>   the past ten years I have had a very good relationship

with Malcolm Cross, both as a student and colleague";
is that right?

Mr Hughes: That is correct, yes.

Ms Kemp: How would you describe your relationship, was it a personal or professional relationship?

Mr Hughes: It certainly started as a professional relationship. I trained at City University where Dr Cross was one of the tutors and one of the course leaders. During that time I had plenty of interaction with him and I sat as a course representative on the Student Council on the course team. We have also sat on various Membership Panels of the Division Committee For Counselling Psychology. I was a press officer of the Division and Dr Cross was a membership secretary when I first joined that. So I knew him as a student, but also as a colleague on those Panels.

It seemed quite straightforward and uncontentious, and Ms Kemp, apparently satisfied she had established the close relation, moved to her next point:

Ms Kemp: If I can then ask you to turn to page 11. At paragraph 3 you refer immediately in the first sentence to the visit to accredit the university's counselling psychology doctoral course ... why were you present at the accreditation visit?

Mr Hughes: At the time I was a member, well, I am a member of the Training Committee in Counselling Psychology, and I recently joined the Committee, and the process is that as you are going through you attend visits as an observer to the process of accreditation visits. I had been a member of the Committee before, but at that point I was there as a student representative.

Ms Kemp: You mentioned that you were part of the Committee, the Training Committee [of the BPS ...], had you ever been on an accreditation visit before?

Mr Hughes: When I was a trainee representative I had been on an accreditation visit. But as I say I had then come off the Committee and I was rejoining.

Ms Kemp: At paragraph 4 on page 11 you refer to a pre-visit meeting ... can you remember when that meeting was arranged.

Mr Hughes: Oh, yes, it was several weeks before I was informed of the process that the visit was going to take at that time, the timings of the various different things that were going to occur. I was informed of the process several weeks before that the visit was going to take at that time, and the timings of the various different things that were going to occur.

Ms Kemp: Who was supposed to be responsible for convening the meeting?

Mr Hughes: Well, the convenor of the visit was Dr Cross.

Ms Kemp: At paragraph 4 you describe that Dr Cross appeared drunk, is that right?

Mr Hughes: That is correct, yes.

Ms Kemp: When did you first notice that fact?

Mr Hughes: Well, as he walked into the bar he appeared slightly unsteady on his feet. But it was when he sat down and started talking it became very clear that his speech was slurred and was actually quite difficult to understand.

When he walked into the *bar*? The next few exchanges try to establish what kind of a meeting this was. We will find out later that Dr Cross arranged for people to meet in the hotel bar at 6.30, phoned Molly Ross to say he'd be late, arrived at 6.45 and left for the restaurant at 7.15 where a table had been pre-booked for 7.30.

Ms Kemp: How would you describe the level of formality of the meeting?

Mr Hughes: I think it was fairly informal in terms of very friendly, people were not sitting round in suits and ties or anything, but it was regarded as a formal part of the visit process.

This ambiguity might possibly be perplexing to a new member of the team, though someone with ten years' experience would probably have taken it in his stride. If Mr Hughes had special questions to raise at the meeting, then these were not mentioned at all. Specific references to real work are completely absent here. Ms Kemp carries on:

Ms Kemp: What was the purpose of the meeting?
Mr Hughes: Before the visit starts we were sent a bundle of papers from the university. The idea is we all read through the papers before the visit, think about any questions we might have, and then ... decide on what questions to ask during the visit. So it is a planning stage for the actual visit.
Ms Kemp: Can you remember how long the meeting lasted?
Mr Hughes: I think it probably finished about quarter past seven.
Ms Kemp: At paragraph 5 and page 11, the third sentence, you say Malcolm Cross did not seem interested, stating words to the effect of this all looks fine; I just want to ask you to what extent you think Malcolm Cross contributed to the meeting?
Mr Hughes: Not particularly. We had met, the other three of us, Simon, Molly, and myself had met at half past six and we had started to go through the papers because Malcolm was not there. We had raised various points we wanted to talk about and were waiting for Dr Cross to appear and take it further. When he arrived he appeared very disinterested. Said, "It is fine, we will move on" as though let's go to the pub or go out for a meal.

Were the questions important or not? What kind of questions needed to be raised at this meeting? No one seems to care less about these matters of detail and work. Later we discover that Mr Hughes was not even a full member of the committee, but was there simply as an observer.

Ms Kemp: If I can ask you to turn, first of all, to page 16 of the bundle. This document is a letter written by you and dated 21 July 2009 ... to the BPS, also copied to the HPC, in which you raise your concerns about Dr Cross's conduct, [if we] turn over the page to page 17, this is a document which is entitled "8 June 6.45 p.m. present: Molly Ross, Simon Parritt, and myself"; [document enclosed with the letter of 21st July 2009]. Would it be right to say this is,

	effectively, a statement that you made for the purpose of reporting the incident?
Mr Hughes:	Yes, I drew up on the evening of the 8 when I got back to the hotel room. It was not intended at that time to be a statement for any particular purpose, but a note of what had occurred that evening.
Ms Kemp:	If I can take you to the first paragraph and perhaps if I read from the third sentence it will show you where I am looking: "Molly tried to take control of the situation and start a discussion about the topics that needed to be addressed at the following day's visit. Malcolm contributed, but appeared disinterested." I want to clarify, if I can, it appears that you say that Dr Cross did contribute in some degree to the meeting?
Mr Hughes:	Well, he was saying I think this is fine. He did contribute. He was not sitting there not saying a word, but the contribution was not terribly helpful in the purpose of the meeting, which was the planning of the visit.

At least, it was not helpful to Mr Hughes, who was there to learn about accreditation visits, but not important enough for him to push his point home there and then in a straightforward way. The question had been easily displaced on the day, only to return with a vengeance a few weeks later in the form of a complaint. It would need to be asked what happened to turn this incident from one that was tolerated into one that warranted a full-blown hearing. I would expect the Investigating Committee to have asked this question, and not to have pushed the case forward without a convincing answer.

Ms Kemp:	If I can then ask you to turn back to page 12 of your witness statement, paragraph 7, you refer then to the group going for a meal in order to get to know each other better, is that right? Had you ever been on one of these social events before?
Mr Hughes:	[yes]
Ms Kemp:	Do you remember how you all travelled to the restaurant?
Mr Hughes:	I believe we all got a taxi.

Ms Kemp: Do you remember how long the meal lasted for?

Mr Hughes: Not exactly. It was a couple of hours probably.

Ms Kemp: I am going to ask you to look at your statement at paragraph 10, page 12. You say that: "Malcolm Cross continued to belittle and pick on Molly Ross in the same way in which he had been earlier in the day. He constantly insinuated that Molly Ross was being a 'spoilsport' and made a big show of paying for the wine himself as Molly Ross, quite rightly, had to keep an eye on the BPS budget." Can you remember what he said specifically on those occasions?

Mr Hughes: I think what was occurring was that—as you can see from the diagram on the other page—Molly set herself aside, as far apart on the table from Malcolm as possible and was spending quite a lot of her time texting on her phone. Malcolm appeared to take objection to that, so was commenting on that and was also saying things like, oh, do not worry I will pay for the wine, you do not need to worry about things, and the tone of voice was suggestive of, as I say, she was being a spoilsport. I think the word "spoilsport" was probably used if I put it in inverted commas in there.

At this point I wonder who was responsible for putting together the case. The booklets point out that the Investigating Committee relies on a paper process, but I had supposed that someone, Ms Kemp, would have spoken to Mr Hughes before the hearing in order to prepare her case. On another occasion I had the chance to ask why that case was presented by an HPC clerk (it was a case proved already via the police, and hence, according to the HPC at least, uncontentious), it was here that I was told that the solicitor was responsible for any further research involved in presenting a case. Today, however, there is a little sense that much investigation has occurred, and this again raises the question of the process that led to this case and to the role of Ms Johnson in this. Unfortunately, the HPC consider this information private, and would not divulge any details when I asked, after the case. The point for now is, shouldn't the HPC know what the facts are before they present the case?

Ms Kemp:	You mention that you confronted him about his behaviour to Molly Ross briefly after that (paragraph 12 on page 13) you say: "As both the night and his drunkenness progressed Malcolm Cross became more and more sexually inappropriate." What stage of the night or meal would you say that this occurred?
Mr Hughes:	This was probably after the main course had been eaten, guessing about 9 o'clock.
Ms Kemp:	Can you guesstimate how long you think you had been there for?
Mr Hughes:	Well, it would certainly be more than an hour we were in the restaurant. Certainly in the early part of the meal I was sat opposite Malcolm, we were having a conversation about various experiences he had been having as a division, Chair of the Division of Counselling Psychology. He had also started talking about other things that were going on in his private life. So that was okay. It was a bit rambling, and it was a bit difficult to follow sometimes, but that was a perfectly friendly conversation.
Ms Kemp:	Did you think at the time that there was a change in his behaviour after the main course?
Mr Hughes:	I think at that point there was an ongoing, when he, as soon as he arrived at the restaurant he was flirtatious with the waiting staff. And what happens after the main course was he became much more tactile with those around him. First of all, Simon who is sitting to his right and then towards me as well.
Ms Kemp:	You have set out in your statement what happened, how did that make you feel?
Mr Hughes:	Well, certainly quite uncomfortable, well, very uncomfortable.
Ms Kemp:	Did you say anything to Dr Cross?
Mr Hughes:	Yes, I made it quite clear his behaviour was inappropriate. I asked him to stop.
Ms Kemp:	You also mentioned some tactile behaviour to Simon Parritt; what was his reaction?
Mr Hughes:	He was just ignoring it, and I think he did say to Dr Cross at one point that is enough or sort of along those lines.

Ms Kemp:	Paragraph 13 and page 13 you describe Dr Cross's behaviour to you, how long would you say that this lasted for?
Mr Hughes:	I think on and off about half an hour probably. It was continuous throughout that period of time.

This is the second ambiguous statement made by Mr Hughes ("on and off" is in conflict with "continuous"), and again goes unremarked.

Ms Kemp:	You mention in paragraph 13 that he attempted, stood up and leaned over the table and attempted to kiss you, do you remember what you did?
Mr Hughes:	I withdrew and put my hand up to make sure he was not able to.
Ms Kemp:	I do not have any further questions for you. But if you remain there, there may be some questions from Dr Cross's representative.

According to this testimony, Owen Hughes has known and worked with Dr Cross for more than ten years, beginning as a student and developing beyond the professional boundary to a more personal relationship as a colleague—he implies that they are on friendly terms yet there is also a dimension of seniority at play in the formal context of the connection. Secondly, he reveals that Dr Cross is responsible for the visit, and that Molly Ross is the administrator. Here the formal aspects of the relationship are more clear, yet there is a power struggle which has its roots beyond the individuals concerned. The modern move to quality management has transformed the traditional meaning of the words and is now beginning to be understood in terms of an ideological struggle for power over work (Travers, 2007)—the quality manager is a rival to the professional over how the job should be done. This overlaps with audit culture, in that today's quality manager uses a different point of reference from the professional, and one that often bears no relation to the reality of the work, but is subordinate to a utopian idea of order. This power struggle is not explored in the hearing. Ms Kemp underlines that Owen Hughes wrote a note to himself directly after the dinner that evening, and later wrote a letter (dated 21 July, three weeks after the transfer of registers from the BPS to the HPC, and six weeks after the event) to the BPS raising his concerns about Dr Cross, copying this to the HPC. The note was not originally intended as an aid to a complaint, but we do not know what happened to affect that transformation. The HPC case is not very clear.

Now Mr Tyme cross-examines Owen Hughes.

Mr Tyme: Just a few questions to ask you on behalf of Dr Cross. How would you describe Dr Cross's character as a person?

Mr Hughes: As a, prior to this event I always had the greatest respect for Dr Cross.

Mr Tyme: How would you describe his character? Is he jovial? Tactile? Is he tactile? You have—

Mr Hughes: I would say friendly, certainly not tactile, but friendly.

Mr Tyme: Would it be fair to describe him as jovial?

Mr Hughes: I am not sure jovial, I am not [sure] what that means, but certainly my experience of him has always been very friendly. He has a sense of humour certainly, and certainly the behaviour I have seen from him previously has not been what it was on that evening.

Mr Tyme: So this was the first occasion that you had witnessed any behaviour of this nature that you refer to in your evidence?

Mr Hughes: It had been a while, probably a couple of years since I had last seen Dr Cross. As I say, I was quite shocked by the change in him, in his behaviour. As I say, I am used to him being a pleasant, friendly, professional person and the behaviour on that night was different.

Mr Tyme: Your attention was drawn to the letter of 21st July 2009.

Miss Reggiori: Page 16.

Mr Tyme: Sorry, page 16.

Mr Hughes: Thank you.

Mr Tyme: A question of clarity, if you look at page 14 at Paragraph 19 your final sentence says: "The ... Society forwarded this complaint to the Health Professions Council on my behalf"; just for purposes of clarity, was it the Society, or was it you that referred the complaint to the HPC?

Mr Hughes: What happened was that at the time this event occurred there, it was when the Health Professions Council was beginning to take over registration of psychologists and I was unsure who the appropriate person to refer this matter to was. So I sent it to the British Psychological Society because at the time I thought they would be the most appropriate people to send it to. I was then informed by them that they were no longer the investigatory body, if you like, of psychologists. They then said that the Health Professions Council were the people to speak to. I had copied that letter to them, the Health Professions Council already, I was contacted, I think, by them to enquire as to whether I wished to make this a formal complaint. At that, yes …

So much for clarity—it seems likely that this period was one of considerable turmoil for Mr Hughes, who doesn't seem entirely sure whether he wanted to make an issue out of this or not. It was also probably a period of great turmoil for the BPS, as it was still negotiating several vital points on the standards to be used once takeover was accomplished.

Mr Tyme: Just turning to the meeting of 8th June, various references to Dr Cross being inebriated to various degrees, can you recall how much alcohol was consumed on that night?

Mr Hughes: Actually during the meal?

Mr Tyme: Yes, well, firstly, let us take it in two stages, firstly, the pre-meeting was there any alcohol consumed?

Mr Hughes: No, no one else was drinking alcohol. I do not think Dr Cross was drinking at that point either.

Mr Tyme: What about the subsequent meal?

Mr Hughes: There was a bottle of wine or two which Dr Cross paid for on the table. He did pour wine for everybody. So I would have thought between the five people around the table I think probably about four bottles of wine were probably drunk throughout the course of the evening. I am not sure that everyone drank the same amount.

Mr Tyme: How would you describe the atmosphere of the meeting?

Mr Hughes: The meeting or the meal?

Mr Tyme: Firstly, the meeting, then the same question in relation to the meal.

Mr Hughes: Well, certainly the meeting became quite tense when it became clear that Dr Cross was obviously drunk. I think it was, initially it was, there was an attempt made to gloss over the fact. Molly Ross attempted to keep it going as if it was normal, but it became very stilted, and I think at that point it was decided that the meeting was probably brought to a close faster than it would normally have been otherwise.

     The actual meal, once we got to the restaurant, as I say, I was probably myself trying to gloss over the fact and was trying to make conversation with Malcolm and with the other people round the table. It was when Malcolm started being unpleasant to Molly that it started to feel quite uncomfortable round the table.

Mr Tyme: Were you aware that Dr Cross had prepared for the meeting, had taken these steps to prepare for the meeting, ultimately the audit accreditation?

Mr Hughes: If he had there was no evidence of it on that evening.

Mr Tyme: Did he not discuss it with you or your colleagues during the course of the meeting? Were you aware he had considered the website of the relevant university and looked at the programme of what was offered?

Mr Hughes: Certainly it was not raised. What he said was that he looked through the documentation and thought it was fine. But that was done in such a way it was difficult, it was impossible to say whether that had occurred or not because it was in such a dismissive manner.

Mr Tyme: But you accept he did say he looked at the documentation?

Mr Hughes: He said that he was not able to comment in any particular detail.

Mr Tyme: How long would you say this pre-meeting lasted? I think you say in your statement he arrived at 6.45?

Mr Hughes: Yes, 6.45 to 6.50. I think we gave up on the meeting by about 7.30 is what I have written on this.

Mr Tyme: When you say "gave up", that suggested that the meeting came to a premature end?

Mr Hughes: I think normally we would have spent a little more time discussing the material. The bundle of material the university provide is substantial, and there was not a great deal of discussion on that at all.

Mr Tyme: What time was the table booked for the restaurant?

Mr Hughes: I could not tell you. I think probably 8 o'clock.

Mr Tyme: You provided evidence as to what you considered to be Dr Cross's role as the convenor, the leader; in relation to Molly Ross what did you consider her role to be?

Mr Hughes: She was there as someone to take notes and to administer the visit, so to book hotel rooms, to ensure that the paperwork was sent out to relevant people. That is my understanding of what her role was.

Mr Tyme: But not necessarily to convene a meeting?

Mr Hughes: No, well, the term "convenor" is applied to the person leading the visit.

Mr Tyme: So there is no dispute according to your statement just dealing with the events which occurred on the following day, the accreditation, that was performed, was exemplary?

Mr Hughes: That was absolutely fine.

Mr Tyme: During the course of the meal, you referred at page 13, "he started to tell me he loved me. He asked me repeatedly to kiss him and he attempted to kiss me et cetera." paragraph 13 of your statement, you were in the presence of Mr and Mrs Parritt, yes?

Mr Hughes: Yes.

Mr Tyme: Did the matters, which you refer to at paragraph 13, did you take those matters seriously? Did you think he, in that context, meant what he said?

Mr Hughes: Yes.

Mr Tyme: That he was going to have oral sex with you?

Mr Hughes: Yes, I was surprised too, but that is what he said and the way he put it made me in no doubt as to his seriousness about that·

Mr Tyme: This is the first time any such comment had been made to you of this nature?

Mr Hughes: Certainly towards me, yes.

Mr Tyme: Could you have misinterpreted what was said here? Could it be viewed as a bad joke?

Mr Hughes: No.

Mr Tyme: So looking at what you describe on paragraph 13 what was the prelude to him wanting to kiss you and offer oral sex to you? Were there any particular comments that he made which foreshadowed that?

Mr Hughes: An element of the conversation I had with Dr Cross that evening was that he had been, he did know I was married because we had a discussion about relationships, and he had been telling me about difficulties with his current relationship. He admitted to a wide variety of inappropriate sexual behaviour, those were the sort of things he was talking about prior to him then saying, you know. I was trying to be understanding and talk about how difficult the time he has had with the Division of Counselling Psychology, the BPS Division of Counselling Psychology, and then at this point he started staying he loved me and we went on from there.

Mr Tyme: Did he also confess his love for Simon Parritt?

Mr Hughes: I think it is entirely possible he did, yes.

Mr Tyme: Did you remonstrate with him as to his behaviour?

Mr Hughes: I certainly did, yes.

Mr Tyme: And it is fair to say that he took heed of your concerns? There did not appear to be any other similar instances?

Mr Hughes: If it is not clear in the statement I apologise, but he tried to kiss me on several occasions, and the rubbing his crotch was also on a separate occasion. So once he had been rebuffed from being able to kiss me he then sat back down and …

Mr Tyme: At what point in the evening was this? Would it be after or before the main meal?

Mr Hughes: This was after the main meal.

Mr Tyme:	By which time a significant amount of wine had been consumed by Dr Cross?
Mr Hughes:	Yes.
Mr Tyme:	I want to now have a look at the morning of the 9th June. You pick that up at paragraph 15 of your statement onwards. What point in time do you first see Dr Cross on the 9th June?
Mr Hughes:	I think what had happened was I had had breakfast and gone back to the room, checked out, I was sitting in the foyer waiting for the other members of the team to appear. At that point Dr Cross appeared and we had a conversation.
Mr Tyme:	Can you recall whether by that stage he appeared to have showered?
Mr Hughes:	He was smartly dressed, but he did smell.
Mr Tyme:	Do you know whether or not he had checked out by then?
Mr Hughes:	I do not think he had checked out because he did not stay there, he went off and came back.
Mr Tyme:	You say he was, he at least appeared sober at this point in time?
Mr Hughes:	Yes.
Mr Tyme:	Turning to paragraph 17 you say on page 14 you agree that Malcolm Cross's behaviour was offensive and reprehensible and that matter had to be taken further; the reference to "we", who is that?
Mr Hughes:	Myself and Molly Ross.
Mr Tyme:	And, again, the decision to refer the matter to the Chair of the Training Committee was whose decision?
Mr Hughes:	My understanding is that Molly had been in contact with her boss from the evening before and she had spoken to her boss who then contacted Allan Winthrop who is the Chair of the Training Committee.
Mr Tyme:	A decision was made then to refer the matter?
Mr Hughes:	What occurred was that following the visit, Allan Winthrop contacted me to say he had spoken to Malcolm who had acknowledged a problem and was dealing with it. It was fine. As I say, this is certainly from my point of view not about punishing Malcolm.

It became apparent that there was a problem. My view is that help would be required. So having had that conversation with Allan Winthrop I was satisfied that help was being sought and that the problem would improve. "The reason I actually referred it to the BPS, with a copy to the HPC at a later date, was that I subsequently found out that (a) there are other people who had concerns about his well-being, colleagues of his at work, and other people who knew him through the BPS. And also that he had joined the Council of the HPC. I had been informed by Allan Winthrop that he was going to take a step back from his academic and professional duties in order to concentrate on getting some help. So when it became clear that he had not followed the advice or taken up the offer of support that he had been offered by his colleague and I believe friend, Allan Winthrop, it then became clear that there was a potential problem.

So, now we begin to get a glimpse of Owen Hughes as a character—he advances himself as a professional friend concerned for a colleague's well-being, but only in so far as it impinges on that colleague's access to powerful positions. The appointment to the HPC Council seems to have come as a particular shock in this scenario, and something that he had to respond to. In his stride now, Mr Hughes throws caution to the wind and really reveals himself by insinuating that Cross's friendship with Winthrop was of the "old boy" type, and therefore is in question, and that there was a faction against him in the field—so much for the wish to help.

> The other issue that came out as part of this is that other people expressed their concerns to me about the way he was working with students and things like that.

Mr Tyme: I do not want to interrupt, but one needs to be careful about straying to matters which are not substantiated in any way.

Mr Hughes: Absolutely. I had concerns that the problem was not being addressed is the short answer.

Mr Tyme: Were you aware that the Society, the BPS, had decided to deal with this matter internally i.e., the matter arising from 8th June? That was the decision that was taken?

Mr Hughes: I am not sure what you mean by the BPS dealing with it internally. As I say, Allan Winthrop informed me that Dr Cross had been told that he would not be taking part in any further accreditation visits. At the time he was still Chair of the Division of Counselling Psychology. As far as I am aware he continued as Chair of the Division of Counselling Psychology until his, the normal term of office ended, which is when I think he then went on to the HPC.

The difference between the way the BPS and HPC handle the same complaint is quite clear and allows us to consider the difference between their respective ideologies.

Mr Tyme: Molly Ross in her statement says, I will quote it to you, it is at page 24, the penultimate paragraph: "We, the Society, considered how best to approach this matter and decided that it could be managed via the Training Committee Chair. I understand that since the accreditation visit, the Chair of the Training Committee in Counselling Psychology spoke to Dr Cross and raised mine and my colleagues" concerns about his behaviour on the visit and Dr Winthrop's comments were received positively'.

Mr Hughes: That was what Dr Winthrop said to me as well. He said he had spoken to Malcolm, and Malcolm had fully acknowledged the difficulties, but the actions did not follow.

Mr Tyme: You are saying his actions, having acknowledged the concerns, did not evidence that he was addressing the issues, have I understood you correctly?

Mr Hughes: Dr Winthrop informed me that he would be stepping back from his professional duties, stepping down as Chair of the Division and those sorts of things. However, that is not what happened. Then, as I say,

> I had a conversation with other colleagues who were equally concerned.

Mr Hughes has forgotten that he has testified that Dr Cross's work at the accreditation meeting was exemplary, and that his performance at the social dinner was unusual. He has forgotten that he wants to help his colleague, and he lets his image slide still further when he appeals to nameless colleagues who, he says, are *equally* concerned, about something as yet unspecified. There is a nameless accusation emerging that gives a pernicious flavour to the proceedings. The date of transfer to the HPC now enters and gives some helpful context:

Mr Tyme:	When you say that is not what happened at what point in time are you referring to?
Mr Hughes:	Certainly when I attended the Division of Counselling Psychology conference.
Mr Tyme:	Which was when?
Mr Hughes:	I think that would have been either the beginning of July or end of June. Certainly no mention was made that any one other than Dr Cross was Chair of the Division, or even acting. Certainly the people I spoke to express my concern that Dr Cross was being helped said they knew nothing of that.

The proceedings are interrupted here with a mass of confusion about where the questions are leading.

Mr Tyme:	This comment that I refer you to by Molly Ross is dated 17th September, which is some time after the time you have—
Mr Hughes:	This is the first time I have ever seen this.
Mr Tyme:	I accept that.
Mr Hughes:	I am not quite sure the context these things are made in.
Mr Tyme:	No, I am trying to establish the timeframe, what your evidence was, you make this complaint, no steps were taken vis-a-vis remedial action.
Mr Russen:	You are asking Mr Hughes about a letter written by somebody else.

Mr Tyme: No, I am not. I am asking—

Mr Russen: You have been.

Mr Hughes: This is a document written by—

Mr Tyme: If I can explain.

Mr Russen: Let me ask you to make something clear because I am getting a bit confused. These questions started on page 24 with that penultimate paragraph, "we, the Society, consider how best to approach", and you have been asking Mr Hughes questions based on this letter. I am not clear in my mind whether you are suggesting that Mr Hughes was a party to the "we" that Molly Ross is referring to in this letter in that passage.

Mr Tyme: No, I think we have moved on from there. The point is this, what Mr Hughes refers to is his complaint of 21st July. He then said the reason why he lodged this matter, referred the matter, was because no appropriate actions were being taken following on from his discussion with Allan Winthrop. I am simply trying to get that timeframe clear. He then alluded to, or he specifically said around June or July, at the end of the conference. I simply pointed out that the comment by Molly Ross in her letter was dated September and it quite clearly says—.

Mr Russen: This was a letter written in September.

Mr Tyme: Accepted. I cannot say more than that. It is written, but it is some—.

Mr Russen: It is not saying we, the Society, considered in September how best to approach the matter. It is just she is recording something in September, something that had clearly happened at some point we cannot from the face of the letter identify.

Mr Tyme: That is fair. It was on 17th September—.

Miss Reggiori: Perhaps those questions would be better addressed to Ms Ross rather than Mr Hughes.

Mr Tyme: That is fine.

Mr Russen: But one pertinent thing that does arise out of this exchange is that you are interested to discover from Mr Hughes an approximate date of when Mr Hughes had his conversation with Dr Winthrop.

Mr Hughes: That was I would have thought 10th June.

Mr Tyme: I think you said June, around conference time, is my note.

Mr Hughes: Let me be clear then. Once the visit had been completed I was phoned a day or two afterwards by Dr Winthrop to first of all express his concerns about what had happened on the visit. This was the first time I had been on a visit as a professional member of the Committee, and wanted to make it clear that this was not normally the way things would have occurred. He said that he had then spoken to Dr Cross who had already acknowledged the difficulties he was having, and Dr Winthrop said he agreed with Dr Cross a way forward, okay. So that was fine.

Several weeks later I attended the Division of Counselling Psychology conference where I spoke to colleagues of Dr Cross and other members of the Division Committee and they said that they were unaware of any steps that Dr Cross was taking, or, indeed, of any things that were, and then actually added further concerns they had which are outside of the remit of this particular hearing. So it is at that point when it became clear that the concerns were not being taken seriously that I referred the matter to, firstly, the BPS and then the HPC. Does that clarify?

Mr Tyme: Yes, I think understand your answer. Just check my notes. I may have concluded. I will check (*pause*) I have no further questions.

Miss Reggiori: Do you have any re-examination?

Ms Kemp: Madam, no.

The next step is for the panel to put their questions to the witness, but first, let's collect together the new information that has been produced. Immediately after this accreditation visit, Mr Hughes and Ms Ross agreed that Dr Cross's behaviour was offensive and reprehensible, and that they should take the matter further. Dr Winthrop, chair of the training committee, and a friend of Dr Cross according to Mr Hughes, spoke to all the parties concerned and assured them that the matter was in hand. Mr Hughes's suspicions were not really allayed, and covert conversations with some colleagues confirmed support for his position against Dr Cross (which then becomes quite opaque and no longer seems to be related to the events of that evening); this gave him confidence to doubt Dr Winthrop's authority and purpose (which seemed to be located in his status as "friend"), and to pursue the matter formally by alerting the BPS, and copying the letter to the HPC. The timing of this letter was not clarified because of the intervention of Mr Russen, but, as the HPC contacted Mr Hughes asking if he wanted to make a formal complaint, we can probably assume that it was written after 1 July (when the HPC took over jurisdiction), after Mr Hughes's private discussions with like-minded colleagues at the annual conference of the Division of Counselling Psychology. This now lands us fairly and squarely in the domain of micro-politics. Which sector of the public is in danger, and from what, or who, at this point?

The Panel are next in turn to question, but only two of them take part. The psychologist has nothing to add (perhaps because there is nothing here that relates to practising psychology, indeed in the whole process he asks only one question). The two lay members are both interested in the same question:

Mrs Alderwick: Yes, if you can help me with one or two things. You say that Dr Cross was very drunk when he arrived at the pre-meeting, you used that expression at least three times that I can find in the various documents, did anyone during the course of the pre-meeting suggest that it might not be a good idea to go to the restaurant?

Mr Hughes: No.

Mrs Alderwick: Did the meal finish earlier than it might have done because of Dr Cross's behaviour?

Mr Hughes: I think it probably did, yes.

Mrs Alderwick: By that I mean did you eat a full meal? You did not leave the restaurant before anyone had finished eating?

Mr Hughes: We had a starter and main course. I do not remember whether we had dessert or not. But I think once we had the main course people felt it was time to leave.

Mrs Alderwick: But it was not abandoned at an obviously early stage? Everyone got fed?

Mr Hughes: Everybody got fed. But I think under normal circumstances we would have sat around talking for longer than we did. It became a bit perfunctory.

Mrs Alderwick: But of the four people other than Dr Cross ... no one was so offended by his behaviour that they left the restaurant; is that right?

Mr Hughes: No one did, no.

Mrs Alderwick: You told us that you remonstrated with him, in fact I think it says in your statement, no, you said in your oral evidence this morning you felt very uncomfortable, you made it quite clear that his behaviour was inappropriate and asked him to stop?

Mr Hughes: Yes.

Mrs Alderwick: If someone is very drunk are they going to be able to take that on board?

Mr Hughes: Yes, he was able to converse. He was not—.

Mrs Alderwick: I think that is a big part of the difficulties I am having, because I am having trouble squaring that with somebody who is very drunk.

Mr Hughes: Well, it depends. I am not sure of the rating scale of drunkenness, but he was certainly disinhibited.

Mrs Alderwick: Yes, obviously.

Mr Hughes: Slurring his speech, but he was capable of coherent conversation, well, vaguely coherent conversation, therefore, he would have, I would have said he was able to follow instructions.

Mrs Alderwick: Can I just ask you if you could look at paragraph 17 of your statement, page 14 in the bundle, the middle of that paragraph it says, "I was also concerned about what I perceive to be a serious alcohol problem", can you tell me what you meant by that?

Mr Hughes: The conversation that I had with him he often refers to occasions where he has been out drunk and behaving inappropriately. Alcohol seemed to play a very large part in those occasions. There was a pattern emerging.

Mrs Alderwick: So those were confessions that were made to you during the course of the evening?

Mr Hughes: Yes.

Mrs Alderwick: The other thing that I just wanted to ask you about is on the previous page on page 13, it is your paragraph 14. This is just for clarification for me, you say: 'I was relieved not only for myself but mostly for Molly Ross who had received the vast majority of his offensive behaviour.

Just reading through this, the examples that you have chosen to include in your statement, most of them do not seem to be directed to Ms Ross. In fact those mostly seemed to have been early on in the evening.

Mr Hughes: I was making reference to my experience of that evening and what had happened to me, three or four things were specific to myself, but there were many other occasions on which he was unpleasant to Molly Ross.

Mrs Alderwick: The last thing, I wanted to return to my first question in a sense, thinking now about this event does it seem wise to have proceeded to a meal in a restaurant where one member of the party was already, according to your description, very drunk?

Mr Hughes: I guess some food might have sobered him up. As I have said before this is not someone who under normal circumstances I would find offensive or aggressive or in any way a difficult person to be with. I think we were saying, well, let's just go with the flow, let's hope it all smooths over ....

Mrs Alderwick: You had that discussion?

Mr Hughes: No, we had not had that discussion.

Mrs Alderwick: Thank you.

The common sense of a lay person reveals the aspects of pseudo-professional speech from the witness ("I am not sure of the *rating scale* of drunkenness, but he was certainly *disinhibited*" ... he was *capable of coherent conversation*, well, vaguely coherent conversation, therefore, he would have, I would have said he was *able to follow instructions* ... Alcohol seemed to play a very large part in those occasions. *There was a pattern emerging*). It also reveals the ambivalence of his position—he seems to want to appear gallant, supporting the parts of the complaint that belong to Ms Ross, while playing down those which affected him. Mrs Alderwick also picks up the retrospective nature of the complaint, which contrasts with the responsibility of all the people concerned. Did they ignore the problem at the beginning? Or was there no real problem at the beginning?

Miss Reggiori: Just a couple of questions, Mr Hughes, was everyone drinking at the restaurant?

Mr Hughes: I think everyone had at least one glass of wine.

Miss Reggiori: Can you remember how much you had to drink?

Mr Hughes: I had two or three glasses of wine.

Miss Reggiori: Can you remember how much Dr Cross had to drink?

Mr Hughes: I could not give you, but it was significantly more than the other people at the table.

Miss Reggiori: Thank you. I have no further questions.

Mr Russen: Just one question which may help the Panel and it is this, have you had any contact with Dr Cross, whether face to face, by telephone, email or letter or in any other way since the validation visit—.

Mr Hughes: No.

Mr Russen: —in June?

Miss Reggiori: Does anyone want to re-examine?

No one did, so Miss Reggiori thanked Mr Hughes and told him he could go.

CHAPTER FOUR

The evidence of the quality assurance officer

In this chapter, we are going to hear the evidence of the quality assurance officer from the BPS. As Ms Ross is a witness on behalf of the HPC, she is questioned first by Ms Kemp. Having established a few administrative details, Ms Kemp opens by quoting from the statement, in which Molly has said:

> I have always had a good professional relationship with Malcolm Cross and felt that his behaviour on the evening in question was entirely out of character.

This is similar to the testimony of Mr Hughes, who also suggests he has a long-term knowledge of Dr Cross against which to judge Dr Cross's behaviour on the evening in question as unusual.

Under questioning, however, Ms Ross is unable to say how long she has known Dr Cross, and cannot be more specific than to say she has worked with him on "just a few" occasions. Ms Kemp and Ms Ross are supposed to be speaking on behalf of the HPC but have produced ambivalent and contradictory evidence in the first moments of their testimony. Ms Kemp moves quickly to her next point, which turns out to be her only point for this witness: "How did Dr Cross behave at the pre-meeting?" This question is borrowed directly from Kelly Johnson, who posed it in a letter to Molly Ross in the run-up to the hearing. Although Ms Ross has already replied, and her reply is in front of everyone around the table in the bundle of papers, Ms Kemp invites her to tell the Panel "in your own words" what she has said.

Ms Ross: These are my own words. He was slightly confrontational towards me. He made a comment that he wished one of my other colleagues had been present, and suggested that they were more fun. He did not conduct the meeting in a way that was required, [and] when I tried to take exception to that [he] made some comments I have noted in the statement there.

Ms Kemp: When you met him at the pre-meeting you describe at Paragraph 1 of the letter on page 22 that he had already consumed a considerable amount of alcohol.

Ms Ross: That was my impression, yes.

Ms Kemp: Why did you form that impression?

Ms Ross: His speech was slurred. He had already suggested going out for a drink. I was under the impression that he was at that time out in town. He also smelt strongly of alcohol.

Ms Kemp: When you went to the restaurant, how did Dr Cross behave towards you then?

Ms Ross: He was quite unfriendly towards me. He made some comments that were belittling. I felt quite bullied. He spoke to me in a very condescending manner.

Ms Kemp: Can you remember anything specifically that he said to you? If you want to, refer to page 23, paragraph 4.

Ms Ross: Yes, I was updating my colleague, my line manager, to update the situation. It was clearly a non-standard evening meal, and when Dr Cross returned to the table he kept asking me if I was twittering, very sorry that I could not be with my friends and I had to keep updating them by text. Also on a couple of occasions when I think Owen Hughes pointed out maybe his behaviour was ungentlemanly and maybe had gone too far Malcolm would turn to me and speak to me in quite a condescending manner asking me whether he had been, had gone too far, had he really.

Ms Kemp: What did you think?
Ms Ross: That he had gone too far.

Ms Ross as a character leaps off the page into life. From her opening stance—"these are my own words"—through to her clear-cut statement that Dr Cross "did not conduct the meeting in a way that was required", and that this "was clearly a non-standard evening meal", we have a glimpse of a true quality assurer. When she says "he was confrontational towards me", we can only wonder at her ability to remove herself completely from the scene so as to avoid the question of what she had done to provoke him. It now seems at least possible that he was teasing her, while she resists the invitation to a comedy and maintains the scene as a drama.

Ms Kemp: Did you observe his behaviour to Owen Hughes?
Ms Ross: I did.
Ms Kemp: Can you describe what you saw?
Ms Ross: For the most part it was friendly and jovial. It was an evening meal that appeared to be between friends, but as the evening progressed Malcolm made suggestive comments, appeared to, well, actually threatened to expose himself and also appeared to try and force Owen to do the same.
Ms Kemp: When you say "suggestive comments", can you remember what they were?
Ms Ross: I cannot.
Ms Kemp: You said that he threatened to expose himself; are you able to describe what he said or did?
Ms Ross: I would not honestly be able to say I could remember it fully. I would not be able to remember the exact phrase or words that were used.
Ms Kemp: You said he appeared to force Owen to do the same, can you remember again what actually happened, spoken or by gesture?
Ms Ross: I think he began to lean forward towards Owen as he was saying something which escaped me. I do not want to suggest something that was said that was not, but the suggestion was that he was asking Owen to expose himself and was making gestures with his hands that he would do it.

Ms Kemp: How would you describe the atmosphere at this meal when
this conduct had taken place?
Ms Ross: I think it was tense, but I would say that Simon Parritt who
was there responded to it in a slightly more jokey and jovial
way. Whereas myself and Owen Hughes responded differently. We were more shocked by the behaviour and taken
aback and felt it was inappropriate.

The table is divided. On the one hand, Parritt and Hughes, who seem to
share an interest in the psychology of enjoyment and sexuality, and, on
the other, Hughes and Ross, who are thrust together on this occasion as
outside that particular interest. The boundary is marked by sex, and perhaps explains why Mr Hughes is compelled to speak of ungentlemanly
behaviour. Ms Kemp then probes a little bit about the purpose of the
meeting, and asks how much Ms Ross had to drink (very little), before
turning to page 24, where her letter to Ms Johnson is reproduced:

Ms Kemp: If I can then ask you to turn to page 24 of your letter, you
say "We, the Society, considered how best to approach this
matter and decided that it could be managed via the Training Committee Chair." Why was that decision taken, do
you know?
Ms Ross: I had a conversation with my line manager, the quality assurance manager, who spoke and progressed the matter up
towards the director of the membership services and support department, and through discussions that they had
also taking into account the situation, and also how Malcolm behaved on the visit itself. It was decided that the best
way to approach it would be to ask Allan Winthrop, who is
the Chair of the Training Committee for Counselling Psychology Division to approach Malcolm and talk through
what happened at the visit.
Ms Kemp: Do you know what the outcome of that conversation was?
Ms Ross: Only by hearsay.

Ms Kemp's case unravels step by step as Ms Ross first of all describes
the meeting in question as friendly and jovial when she should be
building a case of bullying, aggression and intimidation, and then says
she can't actually remember what was supposed to have happened to

upset Owen Hughes so much, then confirms that the dinner has no other function than to eat, and finally reveals she doesn't really know what happened next. She hands the action over to Mr Tyme, who might be expected to make mincemeat of so ambivalent a witness.

Mr Tyme: Thank you. How would you describe Dr Cross's character from your interactions with him.

Ms Ross: —very friendly, happy, very jokey, a very bubbly personality.

Mr Tyme: Had you ever witnessed the kind of behaviour you complained of before from him?

Ms Ross: No.

Mr Tyme: In relation to the involvement of alcohol throughout the evening, would you say generally that alcohol had a significant influence on his behaviour from your impression?

Ms Ross: I would, yes.

Mr Tyme: How many accreditation visits have you attended with Dr Cross before? Can you recall approximately?

Ms Ross: This might have been the only occasion. I do a number of these a year. We might have worked together on an accreditation visit before. We might not have done. To the best of my recollection I attended one other counselling psychology, it might have been two. I am sorry.

Mr Tyme: Just approximately.

Ms Ross: I do so many. This might be the first occasion that we did an accreditation visit together. I might do twenty in a year and I work with between two and three different psychologists each time, so I am afraid I cannot recall.

First point to Mr Tyme.

Mr Tyme: You said in describing Dr Cross's behaviour that he tried to force Owen Hughes to expose himself?

Ms Ross: (*Witness nodded*).

Mr Tyme: Is it that the situation, if I can describe it, he was egging him on if I can put it that way? Encouraging him?

Ms Ross: I would say yes, but also to the point where he leant across the table, it was suggestive that he would help Owen in doing so.

Mr Tyme: Did you view that suggestion as being a serious suggestion having regard to the context within which it was made?

Ms Ross: No, I do not think that it was. I do not know that it would happen, but the suggestion itself I think was inappropriate.

Mr Tyme: So would you agree that the way it was received was possibly not the way it was intended.

Ms Ross: I do not think I would agree with that statement, no. I think it was meant to be jokey, but the situation had already gotten to a point that it was quite clear it had moved on from that, which is why I think, and I can only say that I think, that Owen took it the way that he did. I certainly found it inappropriate. I think that Owen found it inappropriate. It had got past the joking stage by that point.

It was no longer a joke but a manoeuvre in a battle between factions. Mr Hughes, however, appears unable to acknowledge that there are factions at play.

Mr Tyme: Possibly was he teasing? Would that be a fair point?

Ms Ross: Yes, possibly.

Mr Tyme then asks some questions about how long the various parts of the evening took up. It is not clear what he is driving at and he does not close with any conclusion before moving on to another comment made in Ms Ross's letter to Ms Johnson.

Mr Tyme: [line 19, p 38] I want to ask you about a comment you make on page 23 of your letter: "Dr Cross proceeded to get more drunk, he made inappropriate comments to the restaurant staff of a sexual nature and made a big deal of ordering four bottles of wine for our party of five." Is that quantity of wine that you refer to ordered during the course of the evening, or at one point in the evening some additional bottles are ordered?

Ms Ross: As far as I can recall there were two bottles ordered at the beginning and two additional bottles ordered.

Again, Mr Tyme does not underline his point, but he seems to be drawing attention to the way Ms Ross had worded her letter to imply an excess which was not so apparent when the details were spelled out. He then moves on to ask questions which again touch on the factions at the table, where the word "atmosphere" functions as a euphemism:

Mr Tyme: So how you would describe the atmosphere of the meeting by the time the main meal had been consumed?

Ms Ross: I think there were two parts of the atmosphere. I think there was quite a tense atmosphere between myself and Malcolm. I think that the atmosphere between Malcolm and Simon remained quite friendly throughout the evening meal, and I think that the atmosphere Malcolm and Owen progressed from one to the other. [sic]

Mr Tyme: Would you say that any of the gestures that you referred to, or comments made by Malcolm that were directed at Owen Hughes, did he make, in general terms, any similar comments towards Simon Parritt or anyone else?

Ms Ross: There was something said towards Simon. I think it might have been joking about going to the toilet together and there was some sort of remark or a gesture with that, but that was mainly directed towards Owen.

Mr Tyme: But was there a time where these comments were directed to Simon, comments of a similar nature?

Ms Ross: Not that I recall. There could have been, but not that I recall.

Mr Tyme: How did the relationship with Simon Parritt and Dr Cross compare with that of Owen Hughes and Dr Cross?

Ms Ross: I think the relationship between Simon and Malcolm was a lot more friendly and jovial. At times maybe even conciliatory, whereas between Malcolm and Owen I think Owen was quite surprised at the behaviour, and so took a step back from that, so it was less friendly.

Mr Tyme: Turning to the events on 9th June, the accreditation visit, at what point did you first meet Dr Cross?

Ms Ross: It would have been in the morning at a time that we pre-arranged to take a taxi to the university. That would have been between 8.30 and 9.15. I cannot remember the exact time. Probably more towards 8.45, 9 o'clock.

Mr Tyme: Was he ready to depart when you first got there?

Ms Ross: Yes, he was.

Mr Tyme: Can you tell whether or not he had showered, collected his baggage et cetera?

Ms Ross: I do not know.

Mr Tyme: At least refreshed himself from the other evening?

Ms Ross: I could not say.

Mr Tyme: You then all proceed to attend the university?

Ms Ross: Yes.

Mr Tyme: And you in fairness your statement on page 24 in your letter you refer in paragraph, if I may to the second paragraph on that page, you say the accreditation, you describe the accreditation as being a voluntary commitment.

Ms Ross: It is.

Mr Tyme: It falls outside normal work commitments?

Ms Ross: Yes.

Mr Tyme: Presumably the members are not paid?

Ms Ross: They are not.

Mr Tyme: You describe Dr Cross's behaviour on the day as being exemplary?

Ms Ross: I would.

Mr Tyme: He carried out the duties and responsibilities of a convenor with due professionalism?

Ms Ross: He did.

Mr Tyme: Going on to the following paragraph to which you refer where you say: "We, the Society, considered how best to approach this matter and decided that it could be managed by the Training Committee Chair. I understand that since the accreditation visit the Chair of the Training Committee ... spoke to Dr Cross"; who is the Chair you are referring to?

Ms Ross: Allan Winthrop.

Mr Tyme: "He spoke to Dr Cross and raised mine and my colleagues' concerns about his behaviour on the visit and Dr Winthrop's comment were received positively"; what do you mean by the "comments were received positively"? What was your understanding as at the time you wrote this letter?

Ms Ross: My understanding was that Allan Winthrop had spoken to Malcolm and pointed out his behaviour towards me and my comments, those of my line manager, the concerns, his own concerns in response to the behaviour that Malcolm displayed towards me and my understanding at the time was that Allan Winthrop had felt that Malcolm had responded to his comments and his suggestions and his offer of support positively. What I mean by "positively" is that, in effect, he made the right noises and made suggestions that steps were being taken to address his working life and also things in his personal life that maybe were a basis for his behaviour on the visit.

Mr Tyme: Just pause there, and so your state of knowledge at the time, 17th September when this letter was written, was that an approach had been made, Dr Cross had been consulted and at least made some positive noises?

Ms Ross: That was my impression, yes.

Mr Tyme: A decision was made at that point in time that the matter was to be dealt by the Committee, by the Society?

Ms Ross: Internally between the Chair of the Committee and Malcolm Cross, yes.

Mr Tyme: So why was the matter escalated? Did you know what changed? It was to be dealt with by the Committee and then it was subsequently referred to the HPC; do you know what happened in the interim?

Ms Ross: Only through hearsay.

Mr Russen: To be clear, Mr Tyme wishes you to answer the question he is perfectly entitled to ask you—what you understood by hearsay because hearsay is perfectly admissible evidence in these proceedings.

For some reason, though, Mr Tyme declines to press his question, and concludes his cross-examination without making his point. It is interesting to notice that both solicitors and the witness over-formalize the situation by assuming that "hearsay" evidence was inadmissible. Mr Russen's advice is to remind them that no such legal restriction exists; having set up an elaborate process, he now has to remind people to be normal. The action moves back to the HPC solicitor:

Ms Kemp: Madam, I have one question in re-examination. You were asked about the approach made by Dr Winthrop to Dr Cross, and you were asked whether Dr Cross made positive noises and you answered "yes"; what, if any, contact did Dr Cross have with you after that conversation?

Ms Ross: I received a note of apology from Dr Cross.
Ms Kemp: I do not have any further questions.

What kind of a witness is this? She thinks Cross is a great guy, she's never seen him act badly before, she can't remember if she's actually worked with him before, she thinks he was probably joking around, she admits that he bought the wine himself and shared it around generously, she admits that she was the only one there who was being paid to be there, the others were there voluntarily. She confirms that when Dr Cross actually led the accreditation meeting the following day, "he was exemplary". She considers herself part of the decision-making machinery that agreed to deal with the problem internally. She had accepted an apology from Dr Cross, yet still agrees to stand as a witness against him at the HPC. Will the Panel help to clarify her position?

Miss Reggiori: [Line 5 P 43] Just one or two questions from me, Ms Ross. You said in response to Ms Kemp, I think, that you raised the matter of Dr Cross's behaviour on 8th June with your line manager?
Ms Ross: I did. Immediately after, when we returned to the hotel. I believe it was about 11.30 pm.
Miss Reggiori: Did you make a written note of what had happened?
Ms Ross: She did.
Miss Reggiori: She did?
Ms Ross: And that is what my letter is based on.
Miss Reggiori: You had access to that note when you answered Ms Johnson's letter of 28th August?
Ms Ross: I did.
Miss Reggiori: Thank you, that is the only question I have to ask.

Mrs Alderwick, the lay Panel member, seems more clearly to be interested in discovering the veracity of Ms Ross's perceptions:

Mrs Alderwick: I have a couple of questions if you could clarify for me, I am not sure I completely understand what happened before the pre-meeting. Did Dr Cross telephone you at some stage?
Ms Ross: He did, yes. I was in the hotel. He phoned me and asked me, he wanted to speak about the pre-meeting,

suggested it was not necessary, asked if I wanted to go out into town. The assumption I made was that it was to go out for drinks but I explained we needed the pre-meeting. I think I might have made reference to Owen in that sentence because he was there as an observer, so to show him how the process of accreditation proceeded.

Mrs Alderwick: Am I right in thinking you told the Panel you gained the impression whilst you were listening to him on the telephone that he had already been drinking?

Ms Ross: Yes.

Mrs Alderwick: From slurred speech or from the content of the call?

Ms Ross: I think from both.

Mrs Alderwick: Then I think, the other thing I am not clear about, first of all, was Dr Cross's behaviour towards you, was any of that sexual inappropriateness directed to you?

Ms Ross: No.

Mrs Alderwick: That was not an aspect of his behaviour?

Ms Ross: No.

Mrs Alderwick: So leaving that completely aside then ... you have talked about his attitude to you being bullying, being condescending and belittling?

Ms Ross: Yes.

Mrs Alderwick: Now, there is a remark that he made about twittering?

Ms Ross: Yes.

Mrs Alderwick: There is a comment earlier on at the pre-meeting to the effect that he said something like "What is your role here?"

Ms Ross: Yes.

Mrs Alderwick: Now, when you write these things down and you take all the context away, I have to say that does not sound like the most offensive thing I have ever read, so what, can you fill in some of the details about why his behaviour towards you was so offensive?

Ms Ross: Yes, it was less about what was said and how it was said. So, for example, I think it was Owen that

	pointed out or said at one point that Malcolm's behaviour towards me had gone too far.
Mrs Alderwick:	This was in the restaurant?
Ms Ross:	This was in the restaurant. At that point Malcolm turned to me and said, "Is it? Have I gone too far?" But he said it in a very condescending way, for example, "Is it? Have I really gone too far? Have I?" It was that kind of, the way things were said rather than what it was that was said. These are the only examples I could think of at the time when I was writing the response.
Mrs Alderwick:	Can you go back towards the earlier part of the evening because obviously the problem had arisen much earlier on, had it not?
Ms Ross:	It had, yes.
Mrs Alderwick:	Can you assist the Panel at all with that in the same way, with the detail, with the tone, with the demeanour, if you like, that accompanied it?
Ms Ross:	It was, again, the tone. In the pre-meeting we started off and it seemed very clear that Malcolm would have preferred my line manager who he has probably more day-to-day dealings with and who is a secretary to the Psychology Counselling Committee. His welcomes and hellos to the other members of the team, also Mr Parritt's wife who was in attendance, were very welcoming, very open, what I would describe as gushing. Told people how nice it was to see them and made a point of leaving me out of that, saying my colleague was more fun. When Malcolm did not direct the meeting, get it started, go through the paperwork or make attempts to go through the paperwork, I intervened at that point and took on the role, and there was a comment made he was convening and Simon was the right-hand man, so what was my purpose in being there. Again, it was all said in a condescending, belittling way.
Mrs Alderwick:	Whilst that was happening in the pre-meeting were you trying to—.
Ms Ross:	Carry on.

Mrs Alderwick:	—keep the business going?
Ms Ross:	Yes.
Mrs Alderwick:	Presumably getting more and more upset—
Ms Ross:	Yes.
Mrs Alderwick:	—by this treatment. Did you consider that it might have been unwise under the circumstances to go out to a restaurant where there would be wine to drink?
Ms Ross:	I did, but I also did not want to leave my colleagues who were also on the visiting team in that situation.
Mrs Alderwick:	Did you ask for their assistance in helping to deal with Dr Cross's behaviour?
Ms Ross:	Not directly.
Mrs Alderwick:	Presumably everybody was aware he was drunk?
Ms Ross:	Yes. Not directly. Owen took it upon himself on a few occasions at the evening meal to make comments. He signalled to me earlier on after the pre-meeting that he was surprised at Malcolm's behaviour and at one point during the evening meal where Malcolm was not at the table and the rest of the team asked me how I was, what was happening, what has gone on. They had obviously picked up on the animosity, the tension between us. But I did not directly ask them for any help.
Mrs Alderwick:	During the course of the meal Dr Cross's behaviour to you was offensive?
Ms Ross:	Yes.
Mrs Alderwick:	But not so offensive that you felt you would leave?
Ms Ross:	Actually, no, I did feel I wanted to leave.
Mrs Alderwick:	Could you have left?
Ms Ross:	I could have, but—.
Mrs Alderwick:	Presumably you had to pay the bill?
Ms Ross:	I did, indeed. I could have left. There was a time when I was almost at the point of deciding to leave and almost to the point of not taking part in the accreditation visit the following day.
Mrs Alderwick:	Then my last question, it is just so I can understand a little better what your perception was at the time of what was happening, you were obviously upset and you were sufficiently concerned about this to report

it very late in the evening to your line manager, was the substance of your concern Dr Cross's attitude towards you or the fact he was drunk?

Ms Ross: I think the concern was about the accreditation visit and how well that would proceed. I think my main concern was that Malcolm would not attend.

Mrs Alderiwck: So you might not have been able to go ahead?

Ms Ross: No, we would have gone ahead, but we would not have gone ahead with our convenor. I thought he would not be present in the morning. That was the impression I got. So my concern for the accreditation visit, as for being upset that was with regard to his behaviour towards me which I think was fuelled by the drink rather than as two separate issues.

Mrs Alderwick: Fuelled by it or caused by it?

Ms Ross: I could not say.

Mrs Alderwick: Thank you very much.

Mr Birkin: I think you have picked up on what was concerned, which was to do with whether there had been any thinking about the accreditation visit. Could you just explain what was the nature of the discussion between yourself and your manager?

Ms Ross: Essentially, I informed her. I told her what had happened during the evening and towards the end I said I was concerned that Malcolm would not be present at the time that we had arranged to be present in the morning at the hotel and that we might have to carry out the accreditation visit without him. We thought about asking Simon to convene, how we might conduct ourselves, how we would explain to the university. Just generally talking through what would happen on the following day and how we would approach that with the team in the university.

Mr Birkin: Thank you.

Miss Reggiori: Any re-examination from either of you?

Ms Kemp: No, thank you.

Mr Tyme: No.

Miss Reggiori: Mr Russen, do you want to ask anything?

Mr Russen: No, thank you.

Mrs Alderwick said that there was no evidence of any bullying or intimidation. Molly could only respond by saying that Owen Hughes thought there was. This was very unconvincing, as indeed was the rest—this was an uncomfortable and disappointing dinner which anyone could have remedied had they given it a moment's thought. No one did anything to help themselves but allowed the irritation to mount. At most, this might be passed off as an organizational issue which could easily be addressed locally.

CHAPTER FIVE

The evidence of Dr Cross

N ow it is the turn of the registrant at the centre of attention. Dr Cross is invited to take the witness seat, and is questioned first by his own lawyer, who establishes that he is who he says he is, and adds the qualifications he has, before launching into the detail. First, Mr Tyme establishes that Dr Cross made the restaurant reservation for the dinner on the night in question and then drew out the details of the accreditation process. In this way we learn that the relevant papers are received about twenty-eight days before the meeting, and web-based documents are consulted before attending the meeting. Was there anything special about this particular meeting? Yes, the accreditation was so close to the HPC takeover that it made sense to conduct the visit with this in mind. However, under the old scheme it was quite normal for conditions or recommendations to be made in the accreditation process, but under the new regime this would mean that the course would not be recognized as one which could pass students onto the HPC register, which would be disastrous for the students and for the university. It was therefore absolutely essential that the university avoid such a catastrophe—they had to pass first time.

Dr Cross: ... So there was an onus upon us to not only bear this in mind, but to be on one level extra-rigorous so as not give the impression that we had not given it due consideration in order to help out in a collegiate sort of way. So there was an interesting situation of being hyper-vigilant in relation to issues and being absolutely satisfied there was nothing wrong. I think that responsibility had been passed down to the course, programme providers because the documentation was exceptional. The best I had ever seen.

Then Mr Tyme established that Dr Cross had accomplished about twenty such visits in his career, and that he liked to conduct them in a developmental way, which is to say

> ... never adversarial, always with a view to trying to assist a provider to deliver the best possible service to the students ... it has very significant consequences, it is absolutely formal. I think there are two perspectives that one can take when one is interviewing or evaluating a particular product. Some people believe that you should put people under pressure to see how they perform under pressure. There is another camp, which I belong to, which is you should make people as relaxed as possible to get the best out of them. So my view is that I would try and put the accreditation team at as great an ease as possible so they could tell their best story.

Now for the problematic question of alcohol:

Mr Tyme: Now, going back to the pre-meeting on 8 June, on your arrival at the hotel had you consumed any alcohol?

Dr Cross: Yes, I had. I had been to lunch. That was prior to setting off from London to Bristol. I recall very clearly having two glasses of wine at lunch with two colleagues who were both working half a day, and had arranged to finish work and have lunch. Then we all went our separate ways.

Mr Tyme: It has been said on your arrival you were drunk, references to slurred speech et cetera, what do you say to that?

Dr Cross: I do not believe that I was drunk. I know precisely how much I drank. It would be extraordinary to be drunk after two glasses of wine.

Mr Tyme: … Mr Hughes raised some concerns about a drink problem, an alcohol problem, are you able to comment on that?

Dr Cross: Yes. I find the accusation extraordinary. I find it extraordinary on a personal level, in that I do not believe I gave him any indication that was the case, and on a professional level I find it extraordinary that [he] could come to a diagnosis, which is in fact what it was, on the basis of a brief conversation.

Mr Tyme: How would you describe your relationship with Owen Hughes? Had you had much contact with him before the 8 June?

Dr Cross: I recall teaching him a very long time ago. I recall teaching him about ten to twelve years ago. He was a somewhat unremarkable student, but really no contact since his graduation from the university except where we may have sat in similar committees. But, again, quite large, so not really a relationship as such.

Mr Tyme: To paraphrase his evidence, if I was to describe him as your confidant, what would you say to that?

Dr Cross: I would not describe my relationship with him as being a confidant or someone whom I was close to, no.

Mr Tyme: But someone that you could tell very personal matters to?

Dr Cross: No, absolutely not.

Mr Tyme: Mr Hughes in his evidence said you told him about your personal relationship; do you recall that?

Dr Cross: I recall that evening very well, and, no, I did not discuss my personal relationship. I believe he is probably talking about my relationship with my partner and I certainly did not discuss my relationship with Mr Hughes.

Mr Russen: Was that challenged?

Ms Kemp: No. It was not challenged—he was not drunk either. (*pause*)

Mr Russen: He has presumably gone, has he?

Ms Dwomoh-
   Bonsu: Yes.

The point disrupts the proceedings—could this have been ironed out in the preliminary process? Is it not the responsibility of the Investigating

Committee to prove the case—that is, to know the strength of the evidence, the value of their witness? Surely someone would have asked what kind of evidence there was that the registrant was actually drunk and then cross-questioned their own witness? What about the Panel and the Legal Assessor—is this not a point at which they might notice that something may have been wrong with the process that led to the hearing? It is the responsibility of the HPC to prove their charge, yet Ms Kemp takes advantage of the situation and actually manages to present it as a problem for *her*, which rather goes against the idea that it is her responsibility to make a case.

Ms Kemp: My note does not refer to those matters including the fact that Dr Cross states he was not drunk. That certainly was not put to Mr Hughes. If I may say, it does present me with some difficulties where a witness's evidence has not been challenged as it should be because I am now not in a position to recall Dr Hughes so that those matters can be put. I would certainly rely on my closing submissions on the fact that these matters have not been put to Mr Hughes and he has not had an opportunity to comment. That will be something that I would ask you to take into account.

But in fairness to Dr Cross it is important that he has every opportunity to present his case and to put those matters to Mr Hughes if his evidence is directly challenged. So it is perhaps a matter for Dr Cross and his representative to consider the difficulty there is that Dr Cross is now giving evidence and should not in normal course speak to his representative either.

Mr Tyme: ... to that extent even if I had put to Mr Hughes was he drunk, he is going to say presumably yes. You have heard from Molly Ross. She has given her account of his demeanour, slurred speech et cetera. I do not think we can take it much further ... Dr Cross has said he was not, or he had two glasses of wine ...

Miss Reggiori: I think the issue, and I am sure I will be corrected by both Ms Kemp and Mr Russen if I am wrong, is you appear to be putting in chief to Dr Cross matters which impact on Mr Hughes's evidence which were not put to Mr Hughes in cross-examination, like, for example,

	whether or not Dr Cross confided in Mr Hughes about his personal relationship which I do not recall being put to [Mr Hughes] in cross-examination.
Mr Tyme:	It may be the manner in which he came out with it. At that stage I would not have had any instruction on that specific point. It came out, he referred to issues of a personal nature. So the question I asked Dr Cross is whether or not he can be described as a confidant.
Miss Reggiori:	Mr Russen, can you assist us with this.
Mr Russen:	I am sorry, I instigated this interruption in Dr Cross's evidence and one thing we should not do is throw Dr Cross off balance by interrupting the flow of his evidence. But there is a general expectation that where a witness against a party gives certain evidence which is not accepted by that party that the respects in which they do not accept it are put fairly clearly to the witness so they can deal with it because it is only in that way that the fact-deciding tribunal, namely the Panel here, can come to a view about it … to be perfectly blunt, it opens the door to Miss Kemp …
Dr Cross:	Could I make a brief intervention, but just to say that I genuinely believe my opportunity to review what was said would be now and not to interrupt at that time. I apologise if I misconstrued.
Ms Kemp:	It is not a matter that I think I can take any further. I think I have expressed my position. I will refer in the closing submissions. It is obviously a matter for both Dr Cross and Mr Tyme as to what they wish to do.
Ms Reggiori:	I think the Panel will need to retire for a couple of minutes.
Mr Russen:	Yes. Ordinarily, Dr Cross, once a witness starts giving their evidence they should not be communicating with their representative. That is the general rule because there is a rule for all witnesses, whether they are Registrants or any other as you probably heard Miss Reggiori say to the earlier witnesses, they should not be talking about the subject matter of the evidence. But I think that it has been accepted that for these purposes if you wish to speak to Mr Tyme about this nobody is going to object.

(The Panel retired from 2.42 pm until 3.15 pm)

I have edited out a lot of the repetition and verbiage to leave the essence, but even so it is clear that there is a great deal of agitation. It is also interesting to note that Mr Hughes has left without knowing the outcome, without hearing what Dr Cross had to say—this hearing is triggered by his letter, after all.

Miss Reggiori: I think unless anyone wants to raise anything [we will] just continue to hear Dr Cross's evidence.
Mr Tyme: Yes.

Mr Tyme now takes Dr Cross to the question of how the conflict played out. Did it happen, did you say the things Mr Hughes complains of? Yes. Why?

Dr Cross: [Line 14 Page 53] ... they were absolutely jovial, silly, obviously now very misplaced. But I was in fact teasing Mr Hughes ... I thought it would have been obvious that this was silliness.
Mr Tyme: Mr Hughes said in his evidence that he took it quite seriously and asked you to stop or control your behaviour—do you recall that?
Dr Cross: I do ... my interpretation [was that] he said this was wrong, was that he understood this to be a joke and he was bored with the joke—.
Mr Tyme: Mr Hughes referred to a sensible discussion he had with you during the course of the evening at some point, rational discussion, can you recall a rational discussion?
Dr Cross: My perception was that all our discussions were sensible or rational apart from when I was in effect teasing him. We did talk about careers and career progression.
Mr Tyme: Mr Hughes described your behaviour as uninhibited as the evening went on. Would you agree with that?
Dr Cross: ... absolutely. I think I am gregarious anyway. I think I am probably much more of an extrovert than Mr Hughes. I think it would be fair to say that I was loud and more animated as the evening progressed.

Mr Tyme then asks about the alcohol—how much was bought, by whom, why. Dr Cross declares that he bought the wine (two bottles to begin, then another two bottles later on) because he thought himself the best-paid member of the party and obviously did not want the BPS to pay for it. The party ended around ten o'clock, by which time he said he was drunk.

Mr Tyme establishes that Dr Cross was not so drunk as to have had no memory of the evening, and then moves quickly to the comments Mr Hughes made about Dr Cross's attitude to Molly Ross. Finally, he underlines Dr Cross's recollection of the accreditation meeting the next day. Dr Cross said he was *curious* about Ms Ross's texting at the dinner table, and had been *surprised* that Mr Hughes had said that he (Dr Cross) was "picking on her". He recalled that the accreditation meeting had gone well, that they had negotiated with the team, and that he had brought Mr Hughes in on the business in order to give him a good experience even though he was there only as an observer. With this established, Mr Tyme tackles the relationship between Mr Hughes and Dr Cross.

Mr Tyme: … Mr Hughes says that he had known you for about ten years, can you just confirm to the Panel the level of interaction you had with him?

Dr Cross: Certainly. I would have taught Mr Hughes. I do not recall precisely when but I would have been in a number of roles. I would have been a lecturer, a programme leader. He would have been one of the cohorts of up to sixty students, sixty to seventy students depending on year. And then he belonged to a Committee which was ancillary to a Committee which I chaired so we would sometimes come into contact, but not directly. But again not a great deal of contact. We did not sit side by side in a Committee that met on a regular occasion. He mentioned being a course representative which would have meant that on at least two occasions a year whilst he was studying at university I would have sat in the same meeting room with him and other students. But that would be the extent of my contact with him.

Mr Tyme: Any social contact?

Dr Cross: No.

And that closes that question for the defence.

Mr Tyme: Your behaviour on the night in question is described by Mr
            Hughes and Molly Ross as out of character. Would you ac-
            cept that?
Dr Cross: It is slightly complex. I do not know how well they know me.

This is a strong point of contention now. Mr Hughes implied that he was
a close confidant of Dr Cross, and Molly Ross said she knew Dr Cross
but couldn't remember if she'd worked with him more than once. This
is something I would have expected the HPC to be convinced of before
recommending the case for such a high profile hearing. The system
appears to allow no room for small acts of common sense.

Mr Tyme: ... Molly Ross in her evidence said that a decision was
            made by the Society to manage the issues which arose out
            of the visit internally—were you made aware of that?
Dr Cross: Yes.
Mr Tyme: As a result of that decision did there come a time where
            you had to take positive steps to address your behaviour?
Dr Cross: Yes, when Mr Hughes made his complaint to the HPC he
            copied in the British Psychological Society, and also my
            employer.

Mr Hughes, as far as we know so far, did not approach Dr Cross directly,
despite believing himself to be his confidant. The information is coming
out in dribs and drabs—there does not seem to have been any thorough investigation beforehand, and no one is keeping a close watch on
the threads of argumentation. What is the function of the investigating
panel? And what role did Ms Johnson play in the process?

Dr Cross continues: [Line 27 P56] So my employer rightly raised this
                       issue with me, and we agreed that we should sat-
                       isfy ourselves that there was no basis to ... men-
                       tal health grounds. That is, Mr Hughes raised
                       the issue of alcohol misuse—a problem with
                       alcohol—and in order to satisfy my employer that
                       there was no such problem I undertook to visit my
                       occupational health physician and staff counsel-
                       lor to discuss the incident and the antecedents to
                       the incident and the incident in the context of my
                       well-being really. So, yes, I did do that.

Mr Tyme: Arising out of your consultations what occurred?
Dr Cross: Well, what occurred is that, well, in the greatest of detail?
Mr Tyme: No, no.
Dr Cross: We have satisfied ourselves that there is no problem with alcohol, and we have done that through engaging in a range of experiments and ongoing consultation.
Mr Tyme: I believe I may have finished. I am going to check through my notes. (*pause*) Just one small point to conclude. Molly Ross recalls something that was said to Simon Parritt—you were joking about going to the toilet together, something of that nature; do you recall that particular comment?
Dr Cross: Not that specific quip. My sense is it was a silly throwaway comment, but not that specific.
Mr Tyme: But you say, you describe it as a quip.
Dr Cross: A quip, I am sure, yes.
Mr Tyme: Those are the questions I have for you, Dr Cross.

Dr Cross appears to be playing a strategic game. He has not suggested that his silliness and flippant remarks were rooted in organizational and theoretical tensions, nor that they were aimed at the incarnation of these differences in the people round the table. He has completely avoided any discussion that would increase understanding of the situation, and has taken the apparently tactical option of passing it off as a bad joke. This helps to explain why his solicitor did not contradict Mr Hughes or Molly Ross on the stand—as Cross has said, he prefers to play a non-confrontational game. This also helps us to understand why he chose to say he was "confused" by Molly Ross's behaviour—the twittering or texting at the table—and not irritated. It is even possible that by using sarcasm he convinced himself that there was no irritation involved—his self-image requires him to "never [be] adversarial" but to act "always with a view to trying to assist a provider to deliver the best possible service".

This looks more and more like a local spat mixed with micro-politics and displaced into the major theatre of an HPC FTP hearing. The failure of everyone involved to think hard about the issue and to permit simple common sense to come into play allows the disaster to roll on.

The next section considers the HPC case against Dr Cross:

Ms Kemp: Dr Cross, if I understand it rightly, you say on 8th June you had lunch with colleagues in London.

Dr Cross: Yes.

Ms Kemp: You had two glasses of wine?

Dr Cross: That is right.

Ms Kemp: And if I understand it right, you are saying you were not drunk when you attended the pre-meeting; do you accept that you were under the influence of alcohol at that stage?

Dr Cross: I had drunk two large glasses of wine and I think that it is reasonable to say "yes".

Ms Kemp: It is just that the evidence of Molly Ross is quite clear and she said she spoke to you earlier in the afternoon on the telephone, would that be right?

Dr Cross: That is right.

Ms Kemp: And she thought that you had consumed a considerable amount of alcohol because your speech was already slurred; do you recall that?

Dr Cross: I recall the conversation. I was on the train at the time and I called her to ask her what time she was arriving. She was already there.

Ms Kemp: And Ms Ross also said in her evidence to the Panel that she thought you were drunk at the pre-meeting; would you disagree with her evidence on that?

Dr Cross: I did not perceive myself as drunk. Again, I am aware of the situation that occurred previously, so I do not want to say she was not telling the truth. I can only say how I perceived myself.

Ms Kemp: Mr Hughes also said that it was his perception that you were drunk, and Mr Parritt, who provided a witness statement, also said that he thought you had been drinking when you attended that meeting; would you accept that, in fact, it might have been you who had misperceived the events and that you may well have been drunk?

Dr Cross: I think to say that I had misperceived events is fairly evident from how the evening transpired.

Ms Kemp: I am just trying to explore whether you are able to fully remember the events because whether you were in fact drunk or not earlier on in your evidence you said that you remembered the evening quite well?

Dr Cross: Yes.

Ms Kemp: In which case you would have quite a good understanding whether you were drunk or not?

Dr Cross: Yes, I think I have been clear in that I said I had drunk two large glasses of wine. I think I was also clear what time I arrived at the meeting. I was also clear who booked the restaurant and how we got to the restaurant. My memory is quite clear of that evening, yes.

Ms Kemp: Would you accept that you were unable to fulfil your function as convenor of the meeting on 8th June?

Dr Cross: I think what is clear is my perception of actually what took place is different to Molly Ross's and also Owen Hughes's. I said that I did not believe that there was a great deal to be accomplished in that pre-meeting because of the state of the documentation and it was my role to determine how to use that time. I did not think it was necessary. I took Molly's point on board that she wanted to go through this procedural or this process in order that Mr Hughes could be exposed to how things were normally done.

Ms Kemp: Was that because you did not think it was necessary or was that because you were drunk?

Dr Cross: It was because I did not think it was necessary.

Ms Kemp: So you disagree with Molly Ross's evidence which was that you were unable to chair the meeting effectively because you were drunk?

Dr Cross: That I did not chair it in the way she thought it should have been chaired is clear, that I was unable to make the decision about whether to have a pre-meeting or not, I made that decision. Whether she believed that to be the right decision or not it is clear from her perspective: not. It was not the decision she would have taken. In terms of the substance of what would have been discussed that is not clear to me. Nor has anyone mentioned any omissions that have taken place of failing to discuss those matters. They are outside my awareness. I hope that goes some way to answering your question.

Ms Kemp: Perhaps if I ask you to look at page 22 of the bundle, at Paragraph 1 Ms Ross is responding to a question "Did Dr Cross appear drunk when he arrived at the meeting on

8 June 2009?" It says there: 'Dr Cross arrived 20 minutes late to the meeting on 8 June 2009. He was charged with convening the accreditation visit, which involves chairing the meeting, taking the team through the institution's documentation and agreeing the questions to be asked at the visit. Dr Cross was clearly incapable of fulfilling his role as convenor. Do you accept that you were incapable as a result of being drunk?

Dr Cross: No.

Ms Kemp: That is despite three witnesses; Molly Ross, Simon Parritt and Mr Hughes saying that you were incapable of chairing the meeting and that you were drunk?

Dr Cross: I am not sure they all said that. I know they all said it was clear I had been drinking and I have said, yes, I had been drinking. I am just not sure if you are familiar with the documentation. There is probably about 700 pages of documentation. There is a time span of approximately 45 minutes. You are not going to go through the documentation. It is up to myself and the Panel, we expect to have read to identify any salient issues that were so pressing they needed to be discussed then. I said very clearly that I did not have any.

Ms Kemp: In relation to the allegation that you were rude, condescending and aggressive towards Molly Ross, do you accept that you behaved in such a way to Molly Ross during the pre-meeting interview?

Dr Cross: What I will say is this, and this is evidence from the very first time I responded to these allegations, I perceived Molly Ross to be a more than reasonable professional person and she is saying that I did. Therefore, I did from her perspective, but that was absolutely not my intention".

Ms Kemp: So perhaps if I ask you to look at what she says that you did. If we turn to page 22 and Paragraph 2. It is probably easier, although I am not going to ask you about this whole section, but if I refer to it. 'In our earlier phone conversation, as noted above, Dr Cross suggested doing away with the evening meeting and had noted his preference for going straight to town. I was able to persuade Dr Cross of the necessity of the pre-meeting, although he referred to it as a chance to "blah blah blah". Dr Cross spent most of his time at the pre-meeting telling the other team members how lovely it was to see them and how much he loved them all. He appeared to have taken exception to me by this point, which I presumed was in response to my declining to go out with him. Dr Cross commented that I was a "different person" and that I was "grumpy" and whispered loudly to other team members that he wished another of my colleagues was there because they were more fun'. If I pause there in relation to that last sentence, do you accept that you said those things?

Dr Cross: Yes, I did.

Ms Kemp: And—.

Dr Cross: —and whispered loudly in order to be overheard. To put this in context I had said repeatedly I did not think this meeting was necessary. You will note later I do ask Molly what her role is. I asked that question in order that she would say "My role here is administrative".

Ms Kemp: We both know that Molly Ross's perception was that your statements were rude and belittling. The Panel has heard her evidence. Do you consider what you said to be rude and belittling?

Dr Cross: I was very, very saddened to read her statement and because it clearly is her view they were and that is really sad.

Ms Kemp: But can you see—.

Dr Cross: I can see why she would be upset because as you read it, it sounds, parts of it sound, awful.

Ms Kemp: You say it was not your intention, but do you accept they were rude things to say?

Dr Cross: I look at the word "grumpy"; if I was trying to be rude and derogatory I would not use the word "grumpy". But someone who hears "grumpy" and takes great offence, I am sorry for that.

Ms Kemp: In respect of the second aspect of what you said, which is also on page 22 and Paragraph 2, if I move on from where I left off: "I tried to keep things moving as best I could, taking up the responsibility for convening from Dr Cross, to which he took exception and asked me what my role was, saying 'I thought I was meant to be convening the visit, and Simon is my right hand man, so exactly what are you here for?'" Do you accept that that was rude and belittling?

Dr Cross: Yes, in retrospect I should have taken her aside and said "I have said twice I do not think we should proceed in the way you want to", but instead I said it in a very clumsy way in front of other people. Yes, I think it is rude.

Ms Kemp: She said that what concerned her most was your tone and that you were sarcastic to her; would you accept that you were sarcastic to her?

Dr Cross: Yes.

Ms Kemp: You said a moment ago that you did not intend to cause her offence, but if you were being sarcastic and you recognise you were being sarcastic you should have recognised that would cause offence?

Dr Cross: I asked a rhetorical question and I think I can understand why she would think I was being sarcastic.

Ms Kemp: Would you yourself accept that you were being sarcastic to her?

Dr Cross: That requires me to reflect on the intention. My intention was not to be offensive. Was I trying to draw attention to things that were happening in the proceedings? Probably, yes.

So the procedure doesn't help anyone get anywhere, but entrenches people in their positions. The audience might draw its own conclusions about character and plot, it might even laugh at the farce of it all. The next section of the transcript gives Ms Kemp plenty of opportunity for pantomime baddie—she seems to enjoy her role of provocateur, missing no chance to spin the story and to paint Cross in the worst possible light. There is, however, some new information that emerges from this process: Dr Cross had apologized to Molly Ross.

Ms Kemp: You have not ever sought to apologize to Mr Hughes for your behaviour, have you?

Dr Cross: No.

Ms Kemp: Why is that?

Dr Cross: I had become aware that Mr Hughes had made a complaint, I did not want to be seen in any way to influence his ability to be able to make such a complaint. I think it is right and proper that anyone can make a complaint against any Registrant at any time.

I think it worth stating the obvious here—that this general statement about the right to complain takes on different hues according to the context the complaint is made in. This is, of course, the question behind this book.

Ms Kemp: But you made an apology to Molly Ross, so why differentiate between the two?

Dr Cross: I did. Molly Ross did not instigate a complaint against me. I knew her manager reasonably well and had had a conversation with her manager after this event where it had become clear to me that Molly was offended by my behaviour. And I thought it was appropriate, at that point it had not occurred to me that she would be giving evidence in which case I might have reconsidered whether I did write to her. I may not have.

A second point to notice is that following an exchange establishing that Dr Cross consulted several professionals at work in relation to possible problems, Ms Kemp asks:

Ms Kemp: Did you think it might be relevant to submit some evidence to show you had done that to the HPC?

There are, perhaps, circumstances in which her question would be pertinent, but in this case it verges on the inquisitorial.

Dr Cross: No, I did not. The reason for that is that I do not believe that my fitness to practise is related to a problem associated with alcohol. If I did, then I would want to provide evidence of addressing that.

I have cut out a chunk of the transcript here, to get to the point where Ms Kemp finally concludes:

Ms Kemp: You are familiar with the standards of conduct, performance and ethics, and I ask you to look at the red booklet in front of you, in particular Paragraph 3. It says: "You must keep high standards of personal conduct, as well as professional conduct. You should be aware that poor conduct outside of your professional life may still affect someone's confidence in you and your profession".

Do you consider that your conduct on the evening of the 8th June met the high standards of conduct expected of you?

Dr Cross: No. Of myself? Absolutely not.

Ms Kemp: I am grateful. I do not have any further questions, but if you remain there, there may be some questions from the Panel.

The Panel ask their questions

Only Mrs Alderwick, the lay member, speaks up. She wants to know what it was that Dr Cross had found confusing about Molly Ross's texting at the dinner table.

Mrs Alderwick: I am probably quite confused about how you are using the word "confusing"—.

Dr Cross: I did not understand why she was doing it because it seemed odd.

Mrs Alderwick: If I am honest, I find it rude that somebody was texting when they were supposed to be having dinner with a group of other people. I would not find it confusing.

Dr Cross: I perceived her to be a professional, quite a professional professional, embodying professionalism. That is why I was confused.

Mrs Alderwick: It is not what you would have expected her to do?

Dr Cross: No.

Mrs Alderwick: That is helpful. An issue that has not been raised, but is mentioned in the documentation, about the day after when Mr Hughes has stated that you smelt of stale alcohol and vomit; is that your recollection?

Dr Cross: Absolutely not.

Mrs Alderwick: Were you ill that night?

Dr Cross: No.

Mrs Alderwick: My last question just so I can fix it in my mind, you are saying to the Panel you were not drunk when you arrived at the pre-meeting, you were drunk at the end of the evening around tennish?

Dr Cross: (*Witness nodded*).

Mrs Alderwick: At what point in that evening did your behaviour fall below your standards?.

Dr Cross: To be frank I should not have had alcohol at lunch because I—giving the impression whether one is drunk, affected by alcohol, clearly had an impact on the way my colleagues interacted. So I would say then.

Mrs Alderwick: So throughout the evening. But you are saying you were not actually drunk at the pre-meeting, but you are acknowledging—.

Dr Cross: I do not believe I was.

Mrs Alderwick: Thank you. That is very helpful.

Ms Reggiori: Is there any—.

Mr Russen speaks up. He wants to straighten out the facts about how and why Dr Cross made use of his workplace's occupational health facilities. Did he do it when his head of department spoke to him?

Mr Russen: There are a couple of points. I think you said in your evidence, Dr Cross, this is towards the end of your evidence in chief, when you were talking about the contact you made with occupational health, you said that that happened because Mr Hughes included your employer in the complaint he made?

Dr Cross: That is right.

Mr Russen: We see the letter of 21st July which is in the bundle was addressed to the BPS, but copied to the HPC and your, I think, head of department?

Dr Cross: That is right.

Mr Russen: Was that, to your knowledge, the first communication with your employer?

Dr Cross: Yes.

Mr Russen: So it would seem to follow from that that your evidence to the Panel is your contact with occupational health was no earlier than 21st July?

Dr Cross: That is right.

Mr Russen: Do you have a copy of the written statement from Dr Winthrop, the one that you handed up to the Panel. I think you should have a look at that because I think there is something in there. If you look at the last complete paragraph on the first page: "I was asked to speak to Malcolm", and then the next paragraph which starts four lines from the end of the page and carries on, if you read those two paragraphs. It could be seen from those that Dr Winthrop's recollection is the agreement to consult occupational health was immediately following the June incident and certainly before 10.10 am on 15th June.

Dr Cross: Two things took place. Firstly, firstly was a period of serious reflection on what had taken place. Then there was the issue of satisfying myself in addition to that reflection that in fact there was no ongoing mental health issue, particularly in relation to substance misuse. That I understood with Dr Winthrop that I would contact the occupational health general practitioner within the university and the staff counsellor, both of whom I had mentioned by name. Then I did do that, and I, there were further conversations that ensued with, initially with my line manager's manager, so the Dean of the School of Arts and Social Sciences. So we discussed the merits of internal consultations with services within and outside the institution. Her view was that—.

Mr Russen: I am going to interrupt you for two reasons, one is my purpose is not to pry into your health matters and to lead you to saying anything about your health you do not otherwise want to say, and also to tell you that it is usual if people do choose to say anything about their health it is usual here to ask the Panel for the purposes of any evidence about a health issue to hold that part of the hearing in private. My question to you was simply directed to the timing of it because I had understood your evidence to be that you had contacted occupational health because of Mr Hughes including your employer in his complaint?

It is hard to imagine how—and where—the line between public and private is being drawn here. The scrupulosity would certainly signify to an audience that something was afoot—it might even raise a laugh.

Dr Cross: The answer is yes to both. I undertook to, and I did. I undertook to Dr Winthrop and I did subsequent.

Mr Russen: Okay. Now, again, I stress that it is not my intention to lead you to say anything about your health, but if you want to say anything about it please flag it up so the Panel can at least consider conducting it in private. When you gave your evidence in chief, you were critical of Mr Hughes. Do you remember you said on a personal level X, and on a professional level that somebody should give a diagnosis and you used the word "diagnosis"?

Dr Cross: That is right.

Mr Russen: It is not my job to defend Mr Hughes, but it may be that what he did was not give a diagnosis, but express a concern, and in that regard I wonder if you care to have a look at another statement that you put before the Panel, that of Mr Parritt. There are two passages here both on the final page, the second page, do you see that middle paragraph, the one that begins "the evening concluded"?

Dr Cross: Mmm.

Mr Russen: The second sentence there discloses that Mr Parritt attempted to call you on your mobile phone a few times, "as my wife and I were concerned that he did not return with us in a taxi and may be at some personal risk, given he had had a lot to drink"; is your recollection of the amount you had to drink by the end of the meal, which is presumably the point when you parted company with Mr Parritt. Was your recollection that your condition was such that somebody might be concerned about your personal safety?

Dr Cross: I recall walking home. The restaurant is a short distance from the hotel.

Mr Russen: Then, again, I will not read this one out, but if you look in the final paragraph, three lines down there is a sentence which begins "I did think". And the final sentence. Do you believe those were misplaced fears on the part of Mr Parritt?

Dr Cross: I do not think there are any grounds for his concerns. You are asking me specifically in relation to that evening then he may well have been concerned I would not be able to get myself back to the hotel safely. That clearly proved unfounded. If we talk about his concerns in relation to a possible problem with alcohol I might have, I would say absolutely unfounded.

Mr Russen: Thank you.

Mrs Alderwick: Can I ask a final question if I can clarify something now in the light of what you have said to Mr Russen. Mr Hughes has told the Panel in his statement that you later said to him you had gone into the town centre and visited a few pubs and bars, are you saying to the Panel you went straight back to the hotel?

Dr Cross: I did. I think that is worth clarifying. In the morning after I had checked out I met Mr Hughes in reception and he asked me had I gone out in town after the evening meal. I thought it was a strange question and rather than say to him "Why are you asking me this?", I went "Yes, yes, yes" and moved on. I can understand now that this looks very strange. But that is why I just dismissed the question, because I did not want to say "Why are you asking me this strange question?"

Mrs Alderwick: In fact you are saying to the Panel you went straight from the restaurant back to the hotel?

Dr Cross: I did. You can almost see the hotel from where the restaurant is.

Mr Russen: Thank you.

Ms Reggiori closes this section and dismisses the witness. She asks Mr Tyme if there is any more evidence, and a colleague of Dr Cross is called in to say what a decent man he is, and that drinking is normal for academics. Everyone has a copy of this witness's statement, and there is a small discussion as to whether it should be made available to everyone or if it should be read out. Mr Russen (in another show of fastidious attention to what should and should not be in the public domain, yet—again—without any clear logic as to why this statement should be read out rather than, say, the statement by Mr Parritt) makes the point that it should be made available. It was not, however, in the pack I received when the transcript arrived. The witness's evidence is a straightforward statement in support of Dr Cross, whom she has known and worked with for ten years. She testifies that he is warm, social, gregarious, tactile, drinks no more than any other academic, and is flirty. Ms Kemp asks her if she thinks he has a problem with alcohol—no more than anyone, she replies. Then she adds:

> I am a member of the Fitness to Practise Panel myself. I would not put myself in a position to support a colleague whose behaviour concerned me. I value my professional career. I value my ethics.

Mr Tyme simply refers to two other statements which he invites the Panel to read, and which are not included in the transcript. These are from the head of department at the university where Dr Cross works, and from Simon Parritt. This marks the end of the day, and Ms Reggiori notes the clock and closes business, reminding everyone to reconvene at ten the next morning, when Ms Kemp and Mr Tyme will make their final statements.

CHAPTER SIX

The final scene

On the second day of the hearing not much new is presented, but it is a full day before the verdict is announced, the Panel having taken five hours to reach their decision. The routine requires us to sit through the summing up by the solicitors. Ms Kemp returns to the three categories (1. Facts; 2. Misconduct; and 3. Impairment) and reminds the Panel that there is a conflict of evidence on several counts, and that they will have to make a decision on what amounts to the facts. She does not remind them that it is up to her to present strong evidence and not up to Dr Cross to disprove her. Dr Cross, she notes, says he was neither drunk nor incapable of chairing the pre-meeting. He says he did not rub his crotch, and that he was making a joke when he offered to kiss and expose himself to Owen Hughes. The questions surrounding Simon Parritt are inconclusive in terms of "fact", but it is, she notes, certain that Simon Parritt was not offended by Dr Cross and that he made no complaint. The only additional point she makes here is that no "truth statement" accompanies Mr Parritt's statement, a position on her part that manages to insinuate that Parritt could be deceitful. She does note that the question of exposure was not something that Mr Hughes mentioned at all in his evidence but was mentioned by Molly Ross, who acknowledged that she was unable to be explicit about it. Given that it is the responsibility of the HPC to make the case against Dr Cross, the case sounds rather weak even if one accepts its underlying premise.

> In respect of the particular of allegation 1(5), namely, that Dr Cross threatened to expose himself, the Council must accept that this was not something which was mentioned by Mr Hughes himself, and that the majority of the inappropriate behaviour in terms of sexual references or touching was aimed at Mr Hughes and it was not something that he mentioned. This was evidence that you heard from Ms Ross and she could not be specific about it. She simply referred to the fact that it seemed as if this was what he was suggesting. So I think the Council must accept that it was not something mentioned by Mr Hughes, and that it was something that Ms Ross only had a more limited view of given her position at the table and her own evidence that this is what she thought was happening.
>
> Moving on then to the particular 1(6), this is that Dr Cross attempted to touch Owen Hughes and Mr Parritt inappropriately. In relation to Mr Hughes, Dr Cross accepts that he leaned over the table in an attempt to kiss Mr Hughes. He stated to you in his evidence that this was a mock situation and that he was being silly. Mr Hughes said when cross-examined that he had no doubt about the seriousness of this situation, in effect, that Dr Cross was being serious. And he said in his evidence "it was the way he put it". Again, in cross-examination when Mr Hughes was asked, "could you have misinterpreted what was said", Mr Hughes said, "it was not a bad joke". His clear response was, no, he could not have misinterpreted it. It was not a joke.

What Ms Kemp says next (which I have edited out) is, in essence, that two people say it wasn't a joke, whereas Dr Cross says it was. She continues:

> You also have to consider motivation in this type of situation. Why would Mr Hughes or Ms Ross come to the Council and state things that they did not believe had happened? They themselves putting themselves through the process of giving evidence in public, knowing that there are ramifications of doing so. I would invite you to consider that. I do not propose to say anything more in relation to the facts.

Ms Kemp poses an important question and pretends the answer is obvious. She places it as if it were rhetorical—but is it? Why would Mr Hughes or Ms Ross come to the Council and give such flimsy evidence knowing that there are ramifications of doing so? Dr Hughes tried to explain his motivation, though in a muddled and contradictory way (to help a colleague he was apparently in league against). But the intention of Molly Ross seems a little like spite, though it would have to be quite strong to explain the trouble she seems willing to go to. It seems likely that there is in fact another actor who is hidden here, but whose motives should really be questioned. Perhaps this actor can be glimpsed by the reference to Ms Johnson—part of the directorate of the HPC itself—left behind the scenes but apparently manipulating things for their own unstated ends.

> But I will briefly then move on to say something about misconduct. Misconduct is not defined as you know in any of the Health Professions Council's orders or rules, or even Practice Notes. It is really a matter for your professional judgement notwithstanding that Dr Cross said that he considered his behaviour was below the professional standards that he would normally keep. It is still a matter for you to determine that. And in a sense you should do that relying on your own experience of what you consider to be proper conduct, bearing in mind what is expected of Registrants of the HPC and I have already referred you to the standard at paragraph 3 of the standards of conduct, performance and ethics.

There is a sense here that Ms Kemp, in spite of her experience at the HPC, is making it up as she goes along. Misconduct is not defined— this in itself is a problem that needs to be addressed and sensible limits set. She says that it is up to the Panel to define it. These three people, appointed by the HPC, only one of whom has gone through the procedures and experiences necessary to qualify as a practitioner, have been granted the power to decide what counts as proper conduct for a fellow human being. What logic underpins this?

> In relation to impairment of fitness to practise, again, the notion of impairment is not defined, but in my submission you can consider it to be a negative, subsisting impact on the registration of a professional who is a member of the HPC.

> There are two elements to fitness to practise, there is the capability element and the suitability element, and the suitability element requires you to consider the wider public policy interests which were referred to the case of Cohen which are referred to in your practice notes, namely, the need to reaffirm clear standards of professional conduct, and to maintain public confidence in a practitioner. Those are the specific purposes or factors that you are considering in relation to impairment.

Again, if we refer back to the practice note, we will see that it contains no details whatsoever of the actual case that gave rise to it. The generalized principle that is drawn from it is therefore ungrounded and left to the whim or wit of the HPC lawyer. It is not a strong argument.

> When considering impairment I would invite you to take into account three factors; firstly, the incident itself, it is accepted that it is a single incident that you are considering. Secondly, I would invite you to consider any insight that you consider has been displayed. And, thirdly, I would invite you to consider the Practice Note of the HPC which sets out some of the considerations which you should take into account when considering impairment. I do not propose to repeat those now, but I should add I was handed the case of Yeong v General Medical Council by the learned Legal Assessor. I understand Mr Tyme was also handed a copy. It is worth mentioning Paragraph 48 of this judgment. This Dr Yeong had been found to have crossed the patient doctor boundary by entering into a sexual relationship with a patient. At paragraph 48 of that judgment, I am not going to read all of it, but I read the second half of it. It says:

> "Where a [Fitness to Practise Panel] considers that the case is one where the misconduct consists of violating such a fundamental rule of the professional relationship between medical practitioner and patient and thereby undermining public confidence in the medical profession, a finding of impairment of fitness to practise may be justified on the grounds that it is necessary to reaffirm clear standards of professional conduct so as to maintain public confidence in the practitioner and in the profession. In such a case, the efforts made by the medical practitioner in question to address his behaviour for the future may carry very much less weight than in a case where the misconduct consists of clinical errors or incompetence."

The text that is being referred to here says: "In July 2002, whilst Dr Yeong was working as a consultant at the Kedang Kerbaul Hospital, a lady (referred to as 'GN') made an appointment to see him in respect of medical complaints. She saw him for consultations again in February and in March 2003. Shortly thereafter, Dr Yeong met GN for lunch. On Dr Yeong's account, set out in a written plea of mitigation to the Singapore Medical Council (SMC) which was also before the FTPP, during this lunch meeting GN propositioned Dr Yeong and suggested they should go to a hotel room together. Soon afterwards they began a sexual relationship. In the course of that relationship, GN insisted that Dr Yeong pay substantial sums of money into her bank account. Dr Yeong paid her 4,000 Singaporean Dollars (approximately £2,000) per month over the course of the relationship, which was continued over about two years, resulting in a total payment to her of approximately £44,000. He also provided her with gifts. GN threatened to expose their relationship to his wife if he did not …" Yeong v General Medical Council, Court of Appeal—Administrative Court, 28 July 2009, [2009] EWHC 1923 (Admin).

http://vlex.co.uk/vid/61505451#ixzz0wwzciqeF

Those then are my submissions in relation to this matter unless I can assist any further.

Miss Reggiori: Is it possible for the Panel to have copies of that decision?

Mr Russen: Yes.

Miss Reggiori: Are you both happy that we should have a copy?

Mr Tyme: I have no objection.

Miss Reggiori: We will find it useful.

Mr Tyme: I will address you on it.

Next, Mr Tyme takes the stage:

Mr Tyme: What I propose to do is respond to some of the points [made] on behalf of the HPC initially and deal with some additional points which I would ask this Panel to consider [as] germane to the final decision. Firstly, I think we ought to refer specifically to the Practice Note so it is clear what is required in such situations. And what is clear from the note is that not every finding of misconduct will necessarily as a corollary lead to a finding that fitness to practise is impaired. And the note expressly states:

There must always be situations in which a Panel can properly conclude that the act was an isolated error on the part of the practitioner and that the chance of it being repeated in the future is so remote that his or her fitness to practise has not been impaired.

I think also bearing in mind some basic overriding principles the other issue to consider is whether or not there is a linkage between the misconduct as a matter of fact and the impairment. You would have obviously such linkage in cases of clinical error and the like. In my submission, this is a more complicated case in that there is no direct linkage between the misbehaviour if I could describe it as such of 8th June as alleged in the allegation and fitness to practise.

I think what we can safely say drink has had, alcohol has had a major part in both how various comments and actions were perceived and also their intention. But for, it seems to me, the presence of alcohol consumed by Dr Cross and some of the other participants there is every likelihood that this matter would not have been referred, be that as it may, it has been.

Dr Cross has candidly made various admissions as to conduct, but I think what is important is the context within which the conduct and/or comments admitted were made. Here we have, essentially, two meetings which, the second meeting with the meal was a social event without doubt. The pre-meeting had a semi-informal, I think was used to describe the meeting by Simon Parritt, semi-informal.

You heard that Owen Hughes had not seen Dr Cross for some time, also Simon Parritt and his wife. It was very much a social context. Comments were made. We see the allegations at (1) to (3), actions at (4) to (7) of the allegations. But what is important if we look particularly at those that relate to Owen Hughes for the moment. Mr Hughes was asked whether or not he considered the actions described in Paragraph 13 as referred to in the allegations were serious, and he accepted his response was, his perception was, they were. He viewed them as such.

You heard from Dr Cross. He said he was being silly, he was joking I think was Molly Ross's words in some instances. I would ask the question of the Panel, this in the context of a public restaurant, were Mr Hughes's conclusions as to the seriousness of what was alleged reasonable? Is it reasonable? Is it likely that there would have been instances of oral sex in a public restaurant? In my submission notwithstanding how Mr Hughes perceived the actions I think we also have to deploy an element of objectivity in making an assessment of whether or not that perception was real or fanciful.

You also heard that in fact Mr Hughes was prepared for the matters to be dealt with internally up to a point and subject to certain caveats. Given the nature of the conduct that he complained of is it reasonable to conclude he really felt it was as serious as it was? As he believed it to be. In my submission it is quite clear that on balance it is reasonable for you as a Panel to conclude this was a bad joke gone wrong and he had overstepped the mark. You have heard various descriptions of his character. I think on balance it is fair to say he is jovial. He is tactile. This was a bad joke not appreciating the sensitivities of the particular individual. That is also relevant to this extent, because Mr Hughes portrays to be, or would like you to believe, someone who is known to have an ongoing relationship with Dr Cross, someone who knows him quite intimately, but the evidence is has not seen him for a couple of years.

You then will or you heard evidence from Deborah Rafalin and Simon Parritt who had a closer ongoing relationship and who know Dr Cross, at least know him much more closely and significantly that Owen Hughes. So I say you must bear in mind the context. It is important the context within which these gestures were made.

Again, reverting to Molly Ross, rude, condescending comments. Again, you heard the evidence from Dr Cross. He accepted the comments. In fact offered an apology direct to Molly Ross after the, a few days after. But it is a question of perception and he was told [to] moderate your behaviour in relation to her and he did. He acknowledged that he may have overstepped the mark, but, again, one's judgement, I think he was described as becoming more uninhibited as the evening went on, which we know can be the effect of alcohol.

In relation to the accounts of Molly Ross and Owen Hughes, Dr Cross has not said they were lying in their accounts. You were asked to consider the motivation, but they could be honest but mistaken witnesses. Mistaken as to what [was] the intent of the comment and/or gesture.

I think, again, that is illustrated in allegation (6), the attempt to touch Owen Hughes and Simon Parritt, you can see how Simon Parritt's evidence [was] alluded to by my friend. He was not troubled being touched, as it were, whatever that meant, by Dr Cross. He said he was never personally offended by anything he said or did. Is that because he had a closer relationship with Dr Cross, a subsisting relationship, whereas Owen Hughes did not? Is it that Owen Hughes in fact was disappointed by the behaviour he saw in Dr Cross? So we do not say necessarily there is any motivation or mala fides in any way, but they can be mistaken … as to interpretation.

Misconduct, you have heard Dr Cross has accepted that his actions fell below the standards that would be expected, and have particular regard to Paragraph 3 of the code of conduct which has been drawn to your attention in recognizing that.

Question of the impairment, and it was described as a negative, subsisting impact on the registration of the member, and you are asked to consider suitability and wider public issues. Firstly, bear in mind, as I have indicated right from the very outset in the Practice Note, this is an isolated incident, the events of 8th June is an isolated incident. And that has been accepted.

Insight, Dr Cross quite clearly thought there may have been an issue surrounding his alcohol consumption, and you heard the evidence, he took steps to attend occupational health and a staff counsellor et cetera just to reassure himself there was not an issue.

Owen Hughes in his statement refers to the potential serious problem, but question—is he in a position to reasonably make that assessment? He had not seen him for a few years. They met for a couple of hours.

On the other hand, you have the evidence of Deborah Rafalin and Simon Parritt. They deal with this issue. So it has been looked at. It has been considered and acknowledged that Dr Cross has taken some steps to address and determine whether or not there is such an issue. There is no more evidence than that before you.

In my submission, he has clearly demonstrated some insight as to if there was a potential problem, it was drink.

Then you were referred to the case of Dr Yeong, which is a High Court case of 8th July 2009, and you were asked to consider Paragraph 48:

Where a [Fitness to Practise Panel] considers that the case is one where the misconduct consists of violating such a fundamental rule of the professional relationship between medical practitioner and patient and thereby undermining public confidence in the medical profession, a finding of impairment of fitness to practise may be justified on the grounds that it is necessary to reaffirm clear standards of professional conduct so as to maintain public confidence in the practitioner and the profession.

What is important about this particular case is, and no doubt you will see it once the case note is handed to you, Dr Yeong was a medical practitioner. He engaged in an inappropriate sexual relationship with a female patient. In my submission it is a clear distinction between Dr Yeong's case on its facts and Dr Cross's case. There is no evidence of any service user and/or patient complaining in relation to Dr Cross or suffering a detriment as a result of his conduct. The Yeong case must be looked at in the context of that particular case. I think the judgment actually says it is one of the most serious breaches that you could commit bringing the profession into disrepute.

The patient, a woman, seduced the doctor, a man, and then bribed him. The implication of sexual predator and hapless victim is somewhat complicated in the Yeong case, and it is not entirely clear what it is that Dr Yeong did to bring the profession into disrepute—was it the bribery, the sex, the deception, or all three that make this case a valid reference point in law? It is certainly a personal tragedy, but not dangerous in any general way (of course there was probably suffering on the part of his wife and children but I'm not sure this is a good reason to prevent a man from earning his living). What is it that makes it a reference point *here*? Is it here as a spectre?

I should also add in this particular case Dr Yeong was also paying a significant amount of money to the patient on an ongoing basis and was almost blackmailed at the end of it. It is a significantly different case. So one needs to be careful as to what parallels are drawn from this case. I would invite you to look very carefully at the factual basis upon which the decision was made.

Continuing with the theme of impairment I think you are entitled, I would submit you are entitled, to take into account the events of the 9th June in looking at the behaviour overall, what steps he has taken since. There is no dispute that the manner in which the accreditation took place on the 9th was variously described as exemplary, without fault. There is no doubt that Dr Cross did what he was supposed to do on the 9th despite doubts as to whether or not he would be fit, awake or what have you. He did, and he did to the best of his ability and [there are] no complaints about what he did on the 9th. It is my submission you are entitled to look at that in looking at considering the question of his impairment, looking forward as opposed to looking backwards.

I also ask you to remind yourself of the evidence that we heard late yesterday in relation to, given by Deborah Rafalin, who is a close friend and colleague who developed a collegiate relationship, professional relationship over the years, and who made it plain to you that she had no qualms in attending to give support, her support in this particular case, and would not have done so had she not honestly believed in Dr Cross's abilities, genuineness et cetera. I would ask you to remind yourself of Dr Rafalin's evidence.

Looking at the issue pertaining to drunkenness which is the first allegation if I can just deal with that. It is accepted by Dr Cross that he had two glasses of wine in London before his arrival in Bristol. Then it is agreed as the night went on his level of drunkenness enhanced. There is no dispute. There is a dispute as to whether at the pre-meeting he was drunk. But you heard evidence that Owen Hughes accepted that Dr Cross had considered various documents and they appeared okay. Dr Cross mentioned 700 pages of documents was the submission. Owen Hughes said there was some discussion which occurred, and Owen Hughes accepted that Dr Cross had made a contribution. It may not have been to the professional standard or to the extent he had hoped, but he had made a contribution. Here you have Dr Cross who has experience of numerous other accreditation visits, as against Mr Hughes, who had attended one such visit previously. But he had looked at the documentation. He had satisfied himself that there were no real issues, accepting that colleague, the purpose of the meeting was to give others an opportunity. But one cannot say that he had not undertaken his responsibility so far as considering the documentation.

The comments, Molly Ross's evidence, she talked also about the tone, the manner in which the comments were made to her as opposed to what was said. It was the manner. Again, one needs to bear in mind the context of alcohol, the influence which alcohol played in this. That may well have affected Dr Cross's manner.

There are not unusual circumstances where people become more confident, more brash. Not to justify the behaviour or the comments, but to explain it and put it in its proper context. I would ask you to bear that in mind.

I should have made a point, do forgive me, in relation to the context, one needs to bear in mind that Simon Parritt's wife was also in attendance at the restaurant. I think that is particularly relevant to the sexually inappropriate behaviour. I apologize for omitting that.

Then ask you to consider the evidence which was tendered yesterday in the form of Simon Parritt and Allan Winthrop. Bear in mind Simon Parritt, whose evidence is referring to the 9th:

I can only say that Malcolm acted in a completely professional way throughout and performed his role as convenor in an exemplary manner without any evidence of alcohol consumption. I understood that what had happened in the interaction between Malcolm and Molly was a serious management issue and as such I expressed this when asked my opinion by the BPS office.

I think that is quite important because in a way it demonstrates the view that was taken of the conduct in relation to Molly Ross, the comments et cetera. Not to belittle the conduct, but to say it was appropriate to be dealt with as a management issue. It was the tone of what he was saying more so than what was being said, and, therefore, it was felt by all other than Mr Hughes, at least latterly, that it was appropriate to deal with it as a management issue. And management issue it may have led to behavioural management training or that type of course.

Unless there are any other matters on which I can assist the Panel, those are my submissions on behalf of Dr Cross.

(*The Panel conferred*)

Miss Reggiori:	Could you just clarify, Mr Tyme, the reason that you raised the issue of Simon Parritt's wife being present, the significance of that?
Mr Tyme:	In relation to, in particular, the sexually inappropriate comments and the reasonableness of Owen Hughes's belief here is conduct, Simon Parritt's wife is present at the table in the vicinity of Dr Cross and others, and it seems to me it is reasonable to submit and contend that

	acts such as oral sex, inappropriate touching et cetera would, in my submission, be unlikely to occur, or less likely to occur in the presence of Simon Parritt's wife. Does that help?
Mr Birkin:	Thank you.
	(*The Panel conferred*)
Miss Reggiori:	Thank you, Mr Tyme. Mr Russen.
Mr Russen:	Right. Dr Cross faces a single allegation and we will come back to the relevance of subparagraphs (1) to (7), but it is a single allegation. The allegation is that his fitness to practise is impaired by reason of misconduct. The seven subparticulars are particulars of the misconduct that the HPC alleges, but they are not seven allegations of impairment by reason of misconduct.

This contradicts Ms Kemp's position ("seven allegations of misconduct"). Mr Russen is here imposing his own correction at the very end of the hearing without making any overture explaining the tack he is taking. It also brings into question his own initiative in bringing the matter of Dr Yeong, whose drinking habits had nothing to do with the case brought against him, into the hearing.

Now, to get to the answer whether this allegation is well founded or not the Panel has to adopt the following procedure. First, it has before considering any other matter to sit down and work out what the facts are. I will come back and say a word or two about each of these three stages in a moment.

But first is the job of sorting out what the facts are. The second is when the facts have been bundled together, the true facts have been bundled together, the Panel then has to say whether the proved facts amounted, note past tense, to misconduct. If, but only if, misconduct is established then the third stage of the enquiry would be for the Panel to consider whether that past misconduct is currently, i.e., March 2010, impairing Dr Cross's fitness to practise. And it is only if the answer to that last stage is, yes, it is, will the allegation be well founded, because absent any affirmative decision along the way the allegation falls and will not be well founded.

Now, in relation to each of those three stages; the facts, the determination of whether facts amount to misconduct, and if there is misconduct, impairment, a word or two. First in relation to the facts, and perhaps this is the single most important matter, the HPC who bring the allegation against Dr Cross have the obligation to prove it. Dr Cross has no obligation to disprove the facts or any part of them, and the standard to which the HPC is required to prove the facts is *the balance of probabilities*, or so that you find that something is more likely than not. The higher standard of beyond reasonable doubt that is appropriate in criminal cases does not apply here.

Now, in relation to hearsay evidence, and hearsay evidence can take a number of forms. It can be a live witness sitting in that chair giving sworn evidence about something they did not directly see or hear themselves. So a witness says 'Bloggs told me X'. That is hearsay, but hearsay evidence can also come in this form, namely the form of the statements of Dr Winthrop and Mr Parritt. That is another form of hearsay evidence. All hearsay evidence is admissible before this Panel. And it is admissible even if it is hearsay upon hearsay. "Bloggs told me that Jones told him that X" and so on.

But, and this is important, when you have any hearsay evidence, whether it is from that chair via a live witness, or in the form of a witness statement, the Panel has to remember when coming to the decision of the weight that can be attached to the evidence that the provider of the underlying statement has not been here to be questioned about what they have said. So the party against whom the evidence is given has not had the opportunity to challenge it, and the Panel has not had the opportunity to explore it. That might, does not necessarily, because it depends what the evidence is, and it depends how the evidence fits with the other direct evidence that you have heard, it might affect the weight you attach to it. That is a matter, like all others, for the judgement of the Panel.

Now, as I have already said, I think this is important, that the consideration of misconduct should not begin until all the facts have been established because it is not seven allegations of misconduct. It is one allegation of misconduct based upon the seven subparticulars.

So the next stage is the assessment of whether any proved facts amount to misconduct. You have to take the bundle of facts for those purposes. Now, the first thing, and perhaps the most important, is that the Panel is not here imposing its decision about what is good or bad or acceptable or unacceptable behaviour. This is a

Panel of the Conduct and Competence Committee of the HPC, and so you will be judging this issue of misconduct by reference to what is appropriate for an HPC Registrant.

Although, in this case, the registrant is less important (there being no reference to the work he does which requires his registration) than his position as a member of the HPC Council.

Now, my suggestion to you is that if the proved facts could not be slotted into one of the standards in this document, the standards of conduct, performance and ethics of the HPC, then it would be very likely not to be HPC misconduct.

Ms Kemp has relied upon, indeed put to Dr Cross who accepted it, I will come back to that in a moment, standard 3, must keep high standards of personal conduct. The Panel might also have to consider number 13, which begins with the requirement to behave with honesty and integrity. And I do not think anybody here is suggesting that Dr Cross has behaved in any way that reflects on his honesty. But it goes on to say, make sure that your behaviour does not damage the public's confidence in you or your profession. It is a matter for the Panel, who will have access to this document, to say, but those are the two that might be relevant.

Now, notwithstanding Dr Cross's acceptance in cross-examination of the breach of Paragraph 3, my advice to the Panel, I think I said this when Dr Cross was asked if he wished to respond to the allegation at the beginning yesterday, it is still a matter of the judgement of the Panel.

Note that both in relation to this issue of misconduct and in relation to the next stage, if we get there, of impairment, the idea of the burden, the concept of the burden and standard of proof is not appropriate. That is fundamental to the assessment of the facts, but once the facts have been established the question as to whether the facts amount to misconduct or if the misconduct is currently impairing are simply judgements for the Panel based on those proved facts.

Now, in deciding whether a proved fact is misconduct the Panel I advise should form their independent view about that, starting with the proved facts which they find. It has been urged upon you by Mr Tyme that you should be influenced by the decision of Dr Winthrop [that] this should be considered as an internal or management issue. I suggest that is not going to be helpful to the Panel. The Panel is going to have to form its view because you are not here as part of the internal management structure of the BPS, you are here as a Conduct and Competence Committee of the HPC, so you have to make your judgement about that.

This point allows us to compare directly the actions of the BPS and the HPC. One deals with the matter realistically, simply and effectively. The other stages an expensive legalistic show in front of the nation's press.

> I am going to venture this opinion because it was something that emerged in the evidence of Mr Hughes yesterday who stated that Dr Cross was a member of the HPC Council. The advice I give to the Panel is not something you have heard from either advocate about, and if either of them wishes to say anything different about this I am sure you would allow them the opportunity to do so, but the advice I give to the Panel is that should simply not weigh at all with you in your deliberation, for the following reasons. If Dr Cross is a member of the HPC Council, as was asserted by Mr Hughes, no higher standard should be applied to him than to any other prac- titioner psychologist simply because he is a member of the HPC Council. So he should not be judged by a higher standard. Equally, he should not receive any favours. This is an independent Panel and your view of this case as it would the case of any other practi- tioner psychologist, any other HPC Registrant. So it is an entirely neutral consideration I would suggest.

If Dr Cross is a member of the HPC Council? *Asserted* by Mr Hughes? This would seem to imply that Mr Russen really is disinterested in the day-to-day business of the HPC. Yet he is there so frequently—and it is not such a big place—it seems strange indeed that he really wouldn't know, or that the rest of the panel wouldn't know, or that anyone in the room didn't know. The fastidious attention to legal correctness is oblit- erating everyday reality.

> [Line 21 p. 14] Equally it is important to focus on this, that it would be the proved facts that amount to misconduct and other Fitness

to Practise Panels, and it happened some years ago with the GMC, who got into trouble with the High Court because they found facts proved, said, in effect, well, those facts do suggest misconduct or lack of competence, but stepped back from that finding because there was a wealth of evidence that in other respects across a wide range of other performance the doctor had performed well. And the High Court quashed that decision. And the basis upon which that decision was criticised is quite clear. It would only be these facts, such of those facts falling between (1) to (7) that you find proved that could lead to the finding of misconduct. And if those facts lead to a finding of misconduct the misconduct finding would not be removed by extraneous considerations.

The GMC case referred to here is not referenced by Mr Russen, so no information can be added to contextualize the danger he is highlighting to the Panel. It seems to hover as a vague threat of some kind. (It is worth noting that Russen is using a High Court quashing as a reference point, something that will become more interesting to us in the final chapter.)

Of course, Dr Cross's general conduct may well be relevant to the next stage, impairment, if you find there was misconduct. Now, there are a number of things to be said about impairment. The first is and also Ms Kemp says there is no hard and fast definition of what it is. And I will venture a suggestion that I think is fairly close to the one she proffered, my version is you should, impairment is most definitely not the same thing as unfitness to practise. And that it is a negative, subsisting impact on a Registrant's capability or reputation, perhaps possibly both.

Now, this is not, I venture to suggest, but I am slightly trespassing into the territory of the Panel by venturing this suggestion, this is not a case of capability because Dr Cross's clinical ability is not questioned in these proceedings. So it is much more to be on the reputation aspect that the Panel would be focusing in considering this question of impairment.

How can the HPC Panel judge whether the profession of counselling psychology has been put at risk?

Now, it may be that it would be difficult to imagine circumstances where a Panel could find there was HPC-relevant misconduct and then say, but notwithstanding the finding of misconduct at the time, there was no impairment because one would seem to go necessarily with the other. But the issue here for your decision is not whether Dr Cross was impaired in June 2009, but whether his fitness to practise is impaired now in March 2010, so nine months later. That, of course, is a different consideration.

Now, the significance of this case of Yeong, of course I will provide a copy for the benefit of the Panel, is this, and let it be said at the outset that, of course, the GMC fitness to practise Panel in the case of Dr Yeong was dealing with a very much more serious allegation than that made against Dr Cross because albeit some time ago, and, indeed, not in this country, Dr Yeong had crossed that fundamental boundary and embarked on a sexual relationship with a patient. Clearly that is not the allegation made against Dr Cross, and the Panel might think the allegation made against him is not only not of that type, but not of that gravity. But the significance of the Yeong case is that it establishes that the Cohen case which is referred to in the Practice Note and to which Mr Tyme has made reference and which he has quoted, that case of Cohen and others, including the case of Professor Sir Roy Meadow, based upon findings that had underlying them issues of clinical errors and incompetence, and the point of the Yeong case is in fact one can demonstrate in the quotation in the HPC Practice Note because there is a passage from Cohen quoted at the foot of the second page of the note. And it says:

As the court noted in Cohen, the sequential approach to considering the allegations means that not every finding of misconduct et cetera will automatically result in a Panel concluding the fitness to practise is impaired as …

There must always be situations where a Panel can properly conclude that the act was an isolated error on the part of the practitioner and that the chances of it being repeated in the future are so remote that his or her fitness to practise has not been impaired.

It is the reference to the word "error" there that gives the clue to the distinction that arose in Yeong and why Mr Justice Sales in that case said there is a distinction between cases founded on clinical

error and competence on the one hand and Yeong type cases
which was not an error, not a clinical error, nor was it incompetence, that it was misbehaviour on the other. And the simple point
is this, that if a finding is based upon clinical, past clinical incompetence then, of course, it is easy to understand a Panel saying that
there is no current impairment if the Registrant takes remedial
steps by the time the Panel is considering the issue, but different
considerations might, do not have to, might apply in a case of pure
misconduct because the additional considerations of public confidence in the practitioner which may not, all a matter for the judgment of the Panel, may not be addressed simply by a finding that
a particular incident would not recur. And that is the significance
of Yeong.

Now, as I have said, the Panel should adopt that sequential
approach rigidly because it is only if that is adopted will the correct answer be arrived at. And as I have already said it will only
be if you not only get to the final stage of considering impairment
which you will not if you find there is no misconduct, but not only
do you get to the final stage of considering impairment and to say
that Dr Cross is currently impaired would you find this allegation
to be well founded.

Now, I will obviously endeavour to help you with any other
matter if I can or if I am asked to by Mr Tyme or Ms Kemp.
As I said, the issue about the relevance or as I have suggested is
an irrelevance of Dr Cross's HPC Council membership is an issue
I have suggested you should hear from Mr Tyme, Ms Kemp, if they
wish to contend something different.

Ms Kemp:	I have no observations to make.
Mr Tyme:	Save to endorse that it is appropriate he ought not to be treated at a higher level of expectation, but …. [*Mr Tyme trailed off here*].
Miss Reggiori:	(*The panel conferred*) "Thank you all very much. I think those closing addresses and Mr Russen's advice to us have been extremely helpful. Obviously, Mr Russen, if we do need further advice we will call upon you".
Mr Russen:	I can hand forward a copy of Yeong. The particular passage to which reference has been made begins at Paragraph 48. It begins with submissions from counsel for the GMC.

Miss Reggiori: We will retire to consider our decision. Obviously we cannot give you an estimate at this stage as to how long we are likely to take. We do not, we are not going to be rushed. It is not fair to anyone if we are rushed, it is not fair to the witnesses who have given evidence, it is not fair to Dr Cross, it is not fair to the rest of the Panel of the hearing. Once we have reached our decision we may well ask the Legal Assessor to assist with the drafting of the decision. But the decision, as he said, is ours and ours alone. Thank you very much for your help so far. I would suggest if anyone wants to go for a short walk we will probably be at least a couple of hours.

         (The Panel retired to consider their decision from 11.16 am until 5.20 pm)

Miss Reggiori: I do not propose to read out the allegations because they have been put to Dr Cross at the beginning of the hearing.

         Dr Cross has attended this hearing and has been represented by Mr Tyme. The HPC has been represented by Ms Kemp.

A single allegation is made against Dr Cross. It is that his fitness to practise is impaired by reason of his misconduct. Particulars of the misconduct are given and are set out in subparagraphs (1) to (7) of Paragraph 1 above. In order for a Panel to decide if an allegation is well founded it is necessary for matters to be considered in the following sequence:

First, to decide what facts falling within the parameters of the allegation have been proved.

    Secondly, to decide if the proved facts amount to misconduct.

    And, finally, if misconduct is established, then to decide if the effect of that misconduct is that Dr Cross's current fitness to practise is impaired.

    The allegation will only be well founded if current fitness to practise is established.

    The Panel has kept at the forefront of its considerations that, save to the extent that Dr Cross has admitted relevant facts, it is for the HPC to prove them. It is not for Dr Cross to disprove the facts or any element of them. The standard to which the HPC is required to prove the facts is the civil standard on the balance of probabilities, namely that something is more likely than not.

Decision on Facts:
The findings of fact made by the Panel are as follows:

1. The Panel finds that Dr Cross had consumed wine at lunch before travelling to Bristol for the pre-meeting. However, the Panel finds that at that pre-meeting in the hotel he was not drunk. Subsequently, after the group moved to the restaurant and further wine was consumed with the meal, Dr Cross became, by his own admission, drunk by the time the group dispersed.
2. Although the Panel finds that there was in fact very little discussion of substance at the pre-meeting, as stated above, Dr Cross was not drunk at it, and accordingly he was not incapacitated by reason of drunkenness.
3. Dr Cross was rude and condescending towards Molly Ross, both at the pre-meeting and subsequently during the meal at the restaurant. The Panel does not find that Dr Cross was aggressive as he was not intimidating or threatening.
4. The Panel finds that Dr Cross made gestures as if he was rubbing his crotch, but that it has not been proved that he actually did so.
5. The Panel finds that Dr Cross did not threaten to expose himself.
6. The Panel finds that Dr Cross did move so as to lean across the table in order to lead OH to believe that he was going to kiss him, but that in doing so he was joking. The Panel does not find that this was an attempt at an inappropriate touching of OH. The Panel finds there was no touching of SP beyond Dr Cross putting his arm around him and that this was not inappropriate.
7. The Panel finds that Dr Cross did make reference in a manner that he believed to be light-hearted to having oral sex with OH. The Panel accepts that in saying this Dr Cross did not in fact intend that his suggestion should be carried out. But nevertheless the use of the words was indeed lewd. The Panel finds that the explanation for the fact that Dr Cross made these lewd suggestions was, as has already been recorded, that he became drunk during the meal.

It follows from these findings that particulars (1) (but only in so far as the restaurant is concerned), (3) (save for aggression) and (7) are proved.

Decision on Misconduct:

It follows that the Panel must consider whether the factual elements that have been proved against Dr Cross amount to misconduct. The nature of the occasion when these events occurred is relevant. It was not a purely professional occasion because they arose in informal circumstances. Conversely it cannot be said it was a purely social occasion because the group was convened for a professional meeting the following day. It is significant that all of the people present at the evening knew Dr Cross and there was no complaint by any third party such as restaurant staff. No issues of public or patient safety are raised by the behaviour. It is not suggested that it forms part of a pattern of behaviour on the part of Dr Cross. Indeed, the witnesses who have given evidence both orally and in writing have stated that it was behaviour that was out of character. This includes Molly Ross who was the recipient of the rudeness and condescending conduct who made clear that it was behaviour that was out of character given her previous knowledge of him.

The Panel fully accepts that if behaviour would justify a finding of misconduct that finding cannot be avoided by evidence of proper behaviour on other occasions. However, the fact that this was an isolated occasion and was accepted by those towards whom the behaviour was directed on this occasion to be out of character is relevant as to how an informed bystander would judge that behaviour. The Panel fully accepts that there can be circumstances in which outrageous behaviour even on a purely social occasion could constitute misconduct on the part of an HPC Registrant. However, having regard to all the circumstances, the Panel has concluded that this particular behaviour on that particular evening on the part of Dr Cross did not reach the misconduct threshold. This is because the Panel is satisfied that it was behaviour that would not damage the public's perception of, or confidence in, Dr Cross as an individual or the profession of practitioner psychologists generally.

It follows from the findings that there was no misconduct that the allegation is not well founded.

And the order is that the allegation is not well founded.

Are there any other matters arising?

Mr Russen: No.

Ms Kemp: No, madam.

Miss Reggiori: Thank you everyone for attending. It has been a very long two days. Thank you all again for your attendance and assistance.

(*The hearing concluded at 5.27 pm*)

Dr Cross ran from the room in tears.

CHAPTER SEVEN

Regulation in action, inaction, or distraction?

The main part of this book is the (slightly truncated) transcript of Dr Malcolm Cross's FTP hearing at the HPC. It is examined in order to think about what the HPC form of regulation means, not because the actions of the man himself are particularly interesting; they are not. The main aim of the work is not to know anything in particular about Dr Cross, although this proves unavoidable—he has been thrust to the front of the picture and hides the real object of our analysis. Nevertheless our purpose is to understand how the HPC realizes its mandate of regulation. By reading this transcript with that aim in mind, it is possible to see behind the man in the dock and to ignore the details of the case and instead to focus on the people, ideas and structures that make up the context of the case, and that turn this into a case, in fact.

I have approached this work as a member of the public—someone in whose name the HPC purports to act but also as someone who has a mundane right, and therefore a duty, to make sure that what goes on around me does not offend. Chris Atkins's film *Taking Liberties* (London: Revolver Entertainment, 2007) was an inspiration in this context. Although the issues that provide the material both in the film and in the book of the same name (London: Revolver Books, 2007) are the more obvious problems relating to the issue of civil liberties (war, terrorism, the arms trade), Atkins focuses on the details and on the experience of ordinary people engaged in small acts of kindness, protest and resistance. Their experience allowed him both to argue how civil liberties in Britain had come under threat as a result of the unprecedented number of laws passed by the government (New Labour enacted "more laws than any other government in history" and "created 3,000 new criminal offences", op cit) and to assess the effect of this legislative juggernaut on the freedoms that have given this country an international reputation for liberty—liberties that many of us have come to take for granted while knowing little or nothing about how they were attained. This theme was also taken up by Raab (2009) and Johnston (2010), whose books offer copious examples of the way in which these new laws are somehow cut off from the logic that might have produced them, and when interpreted locally come to play havoc with ordinary people's lives. Each example given in those books and films demonstrates how the laws passed in Parliament take little or no account of the human factor needed to make realistic, ethical, or even sensible use of the rules.

An especially powerful scene in Atkins's film shows "Old Labour" stalwart Walter Wolfgang (born in 1923) being lifted out of his seat by two security men and ejected from the Labour Party Conference in 2005 for having had the temerity to shout "nonsense" during Jack Straw's speech about the war in Iraq. A younger man sitting nearby (Steve Forrest, a union official) said "Leave the old man alone" and got himself bundled out the door and "actually pummelled" (Atkins, Bee & Button, 2007, p. 22) for having attempted to intervene on the older man's behalf. The film then cuts to Tony Blair, who says "this obviously should not have happened" and then, as if by way of exculpation, adds: "I wasn't in the room at the time".

While we might gasp at the childishness of Blair's disclaimer, it might be more useful to ask why and how those who are "in the room" bring such unnecessary, and apparently unintended, eventualities to life? What has happened to the ability of people to think rationally and to offer small protest against unreasonable orders? The answer proposed by Atkins, Raab, and Johnston, among others, is, of course, that it is the kinds of changes in the structures of power that we are witnessing that seem to compel certain acts. It is as if the new structures make it less easy for "a few good men and women" to act. The structures provide a kind of stage, a set of reference points, which give preference to certain kinds of actions.

At Dr Cross's FTP hearing we saw the legal assessor circulating a ruling relating to a doctor in Singapore who had been blackmailed by a patient with whom he was having an affair. The Singapore case bore no relation to the specifics of the hearing—so why was it used? Was it simply ready to hand and (for reasons that no disinterested and reasonably well educated outsider could even begin to deduce) somehow satisfied the legal assessor's need to inject a semblance of rationality into a case produced from chaos by introducing something that looked like a precedent?

By tracing the birth of the HPC it seems pretty clear that it is a castle in the air, generated by an idea without genuine substance (that professionals are dangerous to the public), given power by a statutory instrument (without proper discussion in parliament), fleshed out by the pen of a lawyer (whose company will make a lot of money from the new organization) and made "real" via appointments to positions of people who either don't or can't ask questions about what they are doing.

Quis custodiet ipsos custodes?

In the rest of this chapter I shall give a series of snapshots of the thoughtlessness of the HPC in action. My examples are drawn from my work over the last two or three years, and much has come from my observations of meetings and hearings at the HPC. We'll begin with the Fitness to Practice systems, before having a look at the new CPD ("Continuing Professional Development") system, and finally the process by which the HPC tried to capture Counselling and Psychotherapy onto the register—this latter takes in the words of people engaged in the meetings that make up the daily life of the HPC.

Fitness to Practise (FTP)

The HPC Annual Report for FTP 2009–10 says: "Hearings where the allegations were well founded concerned only 0.09 per cent of registrants on the HPC Register" (p. 36). This is a very small number. Looking back to 2005–6 there was 1 case presented to the FTP Panel which was declared "not well founded". This accounted 2 per cent of all cases heard that year. In 2007–8 the number of cases not well founded was up to 26, which was 17 per cent of all cases heard that year. In 2009–10 it was 30 per cent (76 cases out of 256): what's happening? Perhaps the Investigating Committee, the stage before the Hearing, has lost control of the quality of cases they refer on, causing an increase in the number thrown out. At one HPC Council meeting I was surprised to hear a Council Member try to spin this as "good news"! But, seriously, what could explain this rise? Perhaps the Investigating Committee is under-resourced, and as the number of registrants increases it is reduced to passing on paperwork when a complaint is received. When I asked if I could observe the process I was told it was "confidential".

Looking elsewhere for clues, I learned that the budget for the FTP Department as a whole in 2009–10 was £6 million, about 40 per cent of total operating costs: a highly significant area of activity. What does the money get spent on? For each hearing, the HPC must pay for the legal assessor (around £600 per day, plus expenses); a stenographer (transcription); administration and photocopying costs; legal services (costs incurred in preparing and presenting cases); Panel members (around £300 per day per person, plus expenses); venue hire (and associated costs); and witness travel and associated expenses. The average cost of holding a hearing (excluding legal services), according to the annual report, is about £4,000 (p. 49–50). The number of cases during 2009–10 was 256 (256 × £4,000 = £1,024,000), which leaves £4,750,000 to be split between legal costs and Investigating Committee.

Although FTP directly affects less than half of 1 per cent of HPC registrants (and less than 0.1 per cent are proven to be actual cases of bad behaviour or bad practice), it uses 40 per cent of the organization's income and justifies the existence of the organisation. The income is raised via statutory instrument from the registrants, but there is no mechanism for registrants to hold the HPC to account over how the money is spent (formally, the HPC is accountable to the Privy Council, not to the people who actually pay for it). This is a sort of taxation without representation.

Cases of incompetence and malpractice are the exception to the rule, yet they soak up 40 per cent of the resources and are presented *as* the rule. This is clearly bonkers—yet underwritten by law. Problems can only follow from this.

At the HPC Council meeting of 10 December 2009, during the Chief Executive's report to the Council, a couple of members expressed their alarm at the increase in FTP hearings (up by nearly 15 per cent). Mr Seale (CEO) smiled and attempted to chivvy things along. He was prevented from ducking the issue quite so easily by one of the newly appointed Council members, Deep Sagar, a management consultant with special interest in prison services, apparently. Seale attempted to laugh it off and said, "If you put a magnifying glass to the paper, then yes, you can see an increase". It was not until Mary Clark-Glass (a lay member of the Council since 2001) suggested that they might need to take on more staff to deal with the increase that Seale took any real notice of the point. He managed to convey, however, the optimism that increased numbers of complaints was a good thing for the HPC (because it validated its reason for being).

There is no mechanism in place to ensure any real thinking is done here; the organization benefits from increased complaints, as does the legal firm that feeds off these cases. The only problem is to get enough new registrants on the books to pay for the process. This problem has now been greatly increased by the Coalition Government's announce-ment that there will be no new professions for statutory regulation.

Although less than half of 1 per cent of all registrants are subject to the FTP process, there is still the question of what might be learned from the content of these cases. Only a very few cases (a percentage of the already small percentage) will relate to behaviour of a genuinely unconscionable nature, where nothing can be learned except the depths to which someone might stoop by using his or her profession to prey on his fellow creatures. Concerning the other FTP cases, it is highly likely that there is something to learn that would be of interest with regard to management practices (a lot of cases are probably symptomatic of organizational dysfunction—something that cannot be addressed by the FTP process) or that has implications for future training in the field.

The HPC milieu is deliberately adversarial and not remotely educa-tional. The lawyers and the Panels are not interested in benefiting from lessons that might be learned from a mistake made in practice, nor in repairing the damage in the relationship with the patient, and the fact that there is only ever one person from the practice on a Panel makes it quite difficult to see how they would bring any wisdom to the wider field via this way of doing things. A complaint received by the HPC is use-ful only as a trigger for action. This is then transformed into a question about fitness to practise in order to comply with the HPC's legal function. Any possibility of addressing the moment of distress and turning the encounter into a productive experience for the patient or the practitioner is foreclosed by this procedure. Any possibility of mediation is obliter-ated by the procedural manual, which designates its use only at the end of the FTP process (by which time neither the complainant nor the reg-istrant wish to speak to each other ever again). By taking the cases out of the professional domain, any and all benefits to knowledge are lost. By removing them from the regional location, it elevates the case into a matter of national concern (clearly nonsense in almost every case). It is as if the process has been specially constructed as a machine for destroying knowledge and spreading ill will (cf. O'Neill, 2002). There can be little doubt that the process feeds feelings of vengeance and even hatred.

On 18 November 2008 I observed a fitness to practise case (FTP01149). This was the beginning of my work when I was not known, and consequently I had been allowed into the room as soon as I had arrived and I was sitting at the back and taking in my surroundings. At the top of the room (upstage), the HPC barrister was exchanging a few words with the legal assessor of the day. She held up a letter from which she read—"It says Mr M has been working for 25 years without a single incident"—and then paused for dramatic emphasis before adding her own word, "reported", to change the meaning completely. They laughed. They knew I was there. The hearing proceeded in the registrant's absence and concluded by striking him off the register. It seemed at least likely that his experience should have been taken into account, and that the Panel might have used a measure of humanity in their deliberations, especially since he had voluntarily removed himself from the register and had given up his work. From the evidence presented that day the registrant's action did not look to me like a confirmation of guilt, but of his despair concerning the fairness of the system. One witness clearly did not realize the scale of the procedure she was participating in, and another was a training manager who seemed anxious to avoid any blame for the actions of this driver. That the panel did not even attempt to understand it from the registrant's point of view made it look very much like another example of what seems to be the HPC's core belief (that the professional has been "getting away with it" for years) overriding its objectivity. The Panel's judgement is published on the internet, where you can read that "the registrant's failure to attend or be represented at the hearing today has meant that the Panel has had no opportunity to consider the registrant's own evidence". Not only does this suggest that the Panel took it as a personal slight that the registrant did not attend, it contradicts the HPC's own documentation, which says "You do not have to go to the hearing but it is generally in your best interests to go" (p. 14 of the pamphlet entitled "What happens if a concern is raised about me?", consulted from the HPC website, February 2011). The Panel also pointed out that it "noted the registrant's statement in his letter that he had worked without incident for a period of approximately 25 years and that he had been suffering from stress at the time of the incident. However, the Panel felt that it could not give much weight to these statements". I did not feel that anything approaching justice was being done here, rather a sort of Kafkaesque flavour pervaded the event.

The first case I observed was that of another paramedic (07913, 5 November 2008). Mr U had worked in the ambulance service for 16 years, 12 of them as a paramedic. He has been registered with the HPC since 2001. Mr U was bringing a woman to the maternity hospital in Liverpool on a quiet Saturday morning. Her baby was in the breech position. As it happened, CCTV had captured the moment of Mr U's downfall on video, which was produced as the main evidence at the hearing. It showed that as Mr U drove through the (almost empty) car park towards the hospital doors, another car was manoeuvring to park. The ambulance did not give way to the car but proceeded to the door of the hospital. The driver leapt from his car (which the camera showed us standing with its door open and its windscreen wipers still going), ran over to the ambulance and hammered on the window and yelled. After a few moments, Mr U got out of the ambulance and using his physical presence and that of a security guard who had come to his aid, backed the gesticulating and remonstrating member of the public back to his car before returning to his work. The employer suspended Mr U (for about five weeks) and conducted an investigation into the incident. Mr U was then sent on a "de-escalation" training course, and returned to work. The HPC, however, was not satisfied, and its representative said "this must be misconduct given the high standards we expect for the profession, therefore you must accept our case and find Mr U unfit for practice". Mr U was represented by his trade union, which persuaded him to take the witness stand. At the time, this seemed to be an unusual and brave act—it was quite a dramatic moment in the hearing. The Panel asked Mr U what had delayed him in conveying his patient to proper care. He answered at length, in a quiet voice, and with a very humble demeanour, and conveyed a lot of relevant information that would not otherwise have emerged from the HCP investigation. Specifically, he repeated that he had made an error of judgement. He showed remorse, made frequent reference to the reflection he had done and the insight he had gotten, and he was able to recite the "correct" procedure (remain in the ambulance and call for help). He also included the information that the camera had not recorded specifically, that the driver of the car was younger and very aggressive and had shouted directly into his face. The panel found that the allegation was not well founded. I bumped into Mr U and his union representative at the HPC gates after the case, and although Mr U looked tired and seemed to be not at all interested in me, I nevertheless decided to speak to them and to explain who I was. They were relieved that I was not a member of the press and would not be snapping their photographs for widespread publication. When I told them that I was particularly interested in the way the HPC worked because it was threatening to capture the field in which I work, Mr U suddenly woke up and in a very alert and focused manner instructed me to work very hard right now to avoid ever being taken into the HPC. He had won his case but seemed not to believe that any justice had been done.

Upon leaving the building after another FTP hearing—this time the registrant was a speech and language therapist—I passed the Panel chairman (Trevor Williams), who was obviously as curious about me as I was about the HPC. He courteously asked me who I was and why I was there before asking my opinion of the case. I said I was surprised that this was a case at all (it was about a young man who had accepted a few pounds in bus fare in return for going a long way out of his way with a treatment). Mr Williams was clearly surprised, but went on to tell me that the Panels were independent of the HPC and had even had their fights to prove it. I believed him to be totally genuine when he gave his heartfelt opinion that this was important work, but when he said that about 5 per cent of the cases they heard really did need to be dealt with in this way, I was baffled. This seemed to be a very small figure, and I thought it undermined his belief in the work that he was doing. Out of the 205,311 registrants (2009–2010) this would amount to thirty-eight cases.

The Panel went on to find that case was not well founded and the young man was cleared of any misconduct. It is, however, worth noting some of the details of this case (No: 01053). It was being held next door to the HPC's offices, in the Evangelical Alliance, whose entrance hall welcomed us in with a quote from Proverbs 16:24—"Kind words are like honey, sweet to the taste and good for your health". When I wrote my notes I reflected on the irony—it was kind words that had gotten this young man into trouble with the HPC. The allegation stated that Mr R provided private speech and language therapy treatment to a client whilst also treating "them" [sic] on the NHS caseload at a Primary Care Trust. I was free to walk down the corridor and to discover for myself that the hearing had already begun. The HPC had only one witness for the case, Ms B, a Band 8a Clinical Lead (internet sources say this is worth £45,000–£52,000 a year) in the NHS. She was also a fairly young woman and had come with a man who seemed to be her father and who made up the other half of the audience that day. Ms B did not know Mr R but had been employed to replace him when he resigned at the end of a sabbatical that he had spent doing good work in a poverty-stricken part of the world. When she took up the caseload, she found one case that had not yet been closed because, it turned out, of purely technical problems. She decided to visit the family to make an assessment. In the course of this visit, the family had been keen to express their admiration of, and gratitude to, Mr R, who had done so much to help their son (a married man in his twenties with Down's syndrome). Mr R had even come and worked with him beyond the NHS-prescribed limit of five sessions. This made Ms B sit up. "Private work?" she said. "But that is not allowed". The family realized they had made some kind of mistake and clammed up. This made her even more suspicious and she wanted to know how much money had changed hands. They stayed silent. I suppose that this young woman's hypersensitivity to how much people are paid and the guilt associated with it, particularly when one works in a publicly funded body, was enough to send her off to the HPC with a complaint. The hearing established that Mr R had been pressed to take his bus fare in order not to offend the family, who did not want to seem to be in receipt of charity. Ms Taheri, the HPC solicitor, argued very strongly indeed that this was a clear case of misconduct and that Mr R should be struck off. Ms B, in a very perverse twist to the protection-of-the-public argument, repeatedly stated that a professional must act ethically to protect himself from suspicion. Ms Hart, on Mr R's behalf, made sure the facts were brought out (which would not have come to light had it been left to the HPC to prove the case), and the Panel threw the case out as unfounded. Mr R had been waiting for this hearing for nearly two years with a question mark over his character all that time. Which part of the public did the Investigating Committee imagine it was protecting in this case? The family whose son received treatment seemed to have been frightened quite considerably when they realized that their gratitude had imperilled a man they wished only the very best for.

This last case (No: 344894) is of a radiographer who works within the NHS, taking referrals from various doctors in the NHS. One day, one particular patient became very disturbed after a "trans-vaginal examination", so much so that she lodged a complaint with the NHS Trust, the Care Quality Commission, and the Health Professions Council. Each of these three organizations undertook an investigation in its own manner, one by one. Each organization, one by one, found that there was no case to answer. The HPC was the last organization to consider this case and had the benefit of knowing that both the NHS Trust and the Care Quality Commission had not upheld the patient's complaint, and of using evidence that had been generated by the extremely thorough work of the NHS Trust. Nevertheless, the HPC chose to advance seven counts of misconduct, none of which was found to be supportable by the Panel when the case was heard (November 2009). The transcript bears witness to the great stress experienced by the registrant, and we may suppose that the patient also experienced a high level of distress that was not reduced by the process (her evidence was held in private, and the transcript is not available). It is not at all clear what benefit was gained by anyone, unless one takes into account the fees paid to the official members of the hearing. It would, however, be important to take into account the expense incurred by the NHS Trust both in terms of sick pay for the registrant (whose experience of the process was clearly unbearable) and the demands on the time of those members of its staff who undertook the in-depth investigations into the allegations.

Continuing Professional Development (CPD)

In the summer of 2008, new legislation passed through Parliament to make certain changes at the HPC. Not only was this the moment that put the psychologists onto the HPC register, and that reduced the Council membership and removed the voting system that had previously been part of the system (there is now no mechanism at all to allow registrants to have a say in how the organization, whose operations and activities they finance, is actually run—there is no real mechanism for anyone to hold the HPC to account, except, that is, the Privy Council), but it also marked the advent of legally defined CPD requirements. CPD is another acronym spawned by the audit culture—it stands for continuing professional development and "at best" is a method of commodifying the way practitioners maintain a link between their qualified practice and ongoing developments in the field. CPD changes the reference point from the reality of work to the arbitrary signs of "output" invented by those whose interest is primarily that of management, itself increasingly divorced from the reality of work that is actually practised (Khurana, 2007). This process shifts the focus from things that inform a practitioner to things that inform a manager where the manager is already more interested in politics (and/or economics) than in the reality of the work itself. It breaks the link between work and worker. It undermines the real reference point (the work) and attempts to impose pseudo-scientific management principles indiscriminately.

The HPC recently decided to get interested in the CPD of its registrants, and now regularly samples a small percentage of each section of the register at renewal time. The 2011 audit of nutritionists found that 100 per cent of all files submitted for CPD check were found to be good. What does this mean? People have either learned how to "make a good return" or have left the field in despair at the lack of rationality. Here is the tale of the way that one practitioner learnt how to make a "good return".

David Smith was one of the physiotherapists randomly selected from the HPC register to submit a CPD file for HPC scrutiny in 2010. He contacted me when he found my HPC Watchdog blog while searching for a way, as he put it, "to understand the powers of the HPC". David has been a physiotherapist since 1992. He told me:

> This is the first time that we are being audited for Continuous Professional Development. It has been made a condition of re-registration that we have to prove CPD activity, and prove how this activity has helped to improve our services. I was selected for audit this year, and duly submitted my CPD activities as per guidelines of the HPC and our Chartered Society of Physiotherapy. However, the HPC has come back to me and said they 'want more evidence how my CPD has contributed to improving the quality of the service'. I pointed out that I am a private practitioner and my patients don't come back if they don't get good quality. I am still waiting to hear from the HPC.
>
> The worrying thing is I have discovered that the HPC says "there is no automatic link between your CPD and your competence. We have a separate process for dealing with lack of competence and this is not linked to our powers to make sure registrants undertake CPD. The Health Professions Order 2001 says that we can set standards for CPD and we can link these standards to renewing registration. We can also take registrants off our register if they have not met our standards".
>
> Alarm bells are ringing!!! I have followed the struggle of the Psychotherapists and Counsellors against control by the HPC and all your posts on the HPC Watchdog website. I strongly feel that

> it is time to curb the powers of the HPC and I am very angry that
> health professionals should be treated like we cannot be trusted.
> I feel that all the health professionals under the umbrella of the
> HPC should get together to fight their corner. Unfortunately, I get
> the feeling from our Chartered Society of Physiotherapy that they
> are all frightened of the powers of the HPC and even tend to take
> their side. It looks like they cannot be seen to take a stance against
> the powers of the HPC.

David felt threatened by the HPC and went on to explain how the audit
had been conducted by one person qualified in physiotherapy and one
who knew nothing of the practice (i.e., in HPC terms, a layperson). Both
of these people had been selected, trained and appraised by the HPC.
The value of a "layperson" involved at this level is not clear, nor is it
clear what "lay" really means here (except that the person concerned
is not a registrant of the HPC). It only makes sense if we bring in the
assumptions behind the political push: that the professionals, if left to
their own devices, would be bound to be dishonest. As it happens, Nick
Clegg is David's MP. He wrote to him, and he communicated with the
Secretary of State for Health, Andrew Lansley, who returned the following information (in David's words):

> Basically, he is saying that the HPC is independent from the profes-
> sions it regulates and from Government "in order to function fairly
> and effectively" and he is therefore afraid that it is not possible for
> the Department of Health to intervene in this matter. He also points
> out the following: "Section 28 of the NHS Reform and Health Care
> Professions Act 2002 gives me as Secretary of State the power to
> make provisions in regulations for the Council for Healthcare Reg-
> ulatory Excellence (CHRE) to investigate complaints about the way
> the nine health professions regulatory bodies have exercised any
> of their functions. However, Section 28 has not yet been enacted
> and the CHRE does not, therefore, currently have any statutory
> power to take action on the complaints it receives. The purpose of
> the CHRE is to promote good practice in regulation and consist-
> ency across the nine healthcare regulatory bodies. In the absence
> of formal powers under Section 28, the CHRE can work with the
> regulatory bodies only informally and consensually on the com-
> plaints they receive". There you have it! The powers of the HPC are
> totally unchecked.

David's problem with his CPD file rolled on. He wrote to Mr Waddle, the *Customer* Service Manager at HPC (another bizarre example of the way words are routinely divorced from their meaning at the HPC—in no way can David be conceived of as a customer of the HPC, and neither, as a matter of fact, can anyone else). He replied, stating that the HPC was still not satisfied, and sent him the assessor's comments:

> The registrant has explained how his experience has improved the quality of his work and how this experience has benefited the service user. The Standards could be met if the registrant can show links as to how his CPD activities within the registration period have *improved* his work and benefited the service user. [emphasis added]

The message has no meaning, yet it comes attached to a standard letter (sent once already to David, stating "you must provide this information within 28 days of the date of this letter. A decision will then be made on whether your CPD activities meet our standards. If you fail to provide a complete profile in that time you are liable to be removed from the Register"). David adds "this effectively means that the HPC have the power to stop me from earning a living without me being able to do anything about it. I find the whole situation distressing ... help!"

The correspondence with David provides another glimpse of the way the tentacles seem to be thrashing around chaotically at the expense of individual registrants. David points out all the anomalies and contradictions that the HPC subjects him to and confirms what I had learned about the lack of any intelligent or wise authority that might hold the HPC to account. This CPD procedure, undertaken in order to "protect the public", threatens to stop him practising and earning an honest living.

I asked David if he had sought help from the Chartered Society of Physiotherapy. He replied:

> They suggested I should try to find somebody whose CPD profile had been accepted so that we can compare or try to submit a profile similar to the example they give for Superintendent Physiotherapists (I am not working in the NHS; I am a private physio). They do not show any sign that they want to fight this, but appear to

be totally submissive and do not want to question the powers of the HPC as if they were frightened to open their mouth. I cannot understand their attitude. (email to author, 4 September 2010)

Finally, on his third attempt, David's submission was accepted:

What I have done is to write my CPD activities in such a child-like way, i.e., I have read this, and therefore learned that, which therefore benefits my patients ... I have just made it fit what they want to hear, i.e., that I have learned new things, when in fact after 18 years of practising there is not much more new stuff out there ... There is no point in writing lengthy case studies and explanations as to how clinical reasoning works because the simple-minded HPC does not understand scientific reasoning. They just want to dumb everybody down to the same level. They also do not communicate whatsoever and move the goal post just as they like. It is definitely not a case of "it does what it says on the tin". They publish guidelines but then do not follow them ... (1 October 2010).

Capturing counselling and psychotherapy (PLG)

I began to become interested in the HPC when it announced the "call for ideas", which closed in October 2008, as the first step in its process to "capture" the field of "psychotherapy and counselling". This process was fraught with difficulties, not least of which was the lack of any demand for HPC regulation from the field, which, on the contrary had made it plain that it thought the HPC a completely inappropriate body for the job. As you might expect in such circumstances, the call for ideas attracted many cogent arguments pointing out the problems that HPC regulation would create for the practice. The HPC, however, presumably preoccupied with the problem of how to manage the annual fees which would accrue (figures which might reach £7.5m), confidently set about following its pre-planned procedure and recruited 11 members to the Professional Liaison Group (PLG). A PLG is the vehicle by which the HPC captures the knowledge it needs from the practitioners in order to formulate a set of "standards". Standards are then used by the HPC and so on during the various FTP, CPD, or course validation procedures.

The members of the PLG for psychotherapy and counselling (P&C) were chosen in the summer of 2008 by an "ad hoc nomination committee" consisting of Professor Diane Waller (then a professor at Goldsmiths College, art psychotherapist registrant of the HPC, and an HPC Council Member) in conversation with Dr Anna van der Gaag (a speech and language therapist registrant, and then President, now Chair, of the HPC) in the company of Michael Guthrie (then acting, now actual Head of Policy and Standards, HPC). They chose (1) Jean McMinn, a counselling teaching fellow at the Queen's University Belfast; (2) Linda Matthews, from the British Association for Behavioural and Cognitive Psychotherapies; (3) Brian Magee—Counselling and Psychotherapy in Scotland; (4) Rose Mary Owen from Relate (her place was in fact taken by Peter Bell); (5) Peter Fonagy, in his capacity to represent Skills for Health (according to the HPC), although Skills for Health defined him more specifically as the Chair of the Psychological Therapies National Occupational Standards National Strategy Group rather than as a representative of Skills for Health per se (email 4 November 2008 to Michael Guthrie); (6) Julian Lousada, Chair of the British Psychoanalytic Council; (7) Sally Aldridge, employed by the British Association of Counselling and Psychotherapy as their Head of Regulatory Policy; (8) Kathi Murphy, a member of the United Kingdom Council for Psychotherapy (Kathi was replaced by Carmen Ablack, Chair of the UKCP Standards Board, and of the Education and Standards Committee, in January 2009); (9) Jonathan Coe, from a coalition of charities purporting to speak on behalf of "the user"; (10) Professor Mick Cooper from the University of Strathclyde, designated as a "personal nomination" and actively implicated in the work of the BACP; (11) Fiona Ballantine Dykes, employed by the Counselling and Psychotherapy Central Awarding Body.

This small group of people were joined by six HPC Council members: (1) Professor Jeff Lucas (Deputy Vice-Chancellor at the University of Bradford and Professor of Health Studies); (2) Eileen Thornton, then the Physiotherapist "Alternate" Registrant Member of the HPC Council and Head of the School of Health Sciences at the University of Liverpool; (3) Professor Annie Turner, Registrant Member of the HPC Council and Professor of Occupational Therapy at the University of Northampton; (4) Mary Clark-Glass, Lay Member of the HPC Council, a General Medical Council associate and a member of the General Dental Council's Fitness to Practise Committee; (5) Graham Smith, Registrant Member of the HPC Council, Fellow of the Chartered Society of Physiotherapy and a Visiting Professor at the University of Teesside (Graham lost his seat on the HPC Council in the big changeover in 2010, and vanished from the PLG); and (6) Chair of the PLG Professor Diane Waller, Registrant Member of the HPC Council and Professor of Art Psychotherapy at Goldsmiths College. Dr van der Gaag was also always present at these meetings, as was Michael Guthrie.

The PLG was scheduled to meet 5 times (4 December 2008, 28 and 29 January 2009, 3 and 4 March 2009, 29 April 2009 and 26 and 27 May 2009) "to discuss, debate, and air the issues" surrounding the questions of structure of the register, protected titles, voluntary register transfers and grand-parenting, education and training and standards of proficiency.

The HPC made it clear that the PLG was "not a decision-making body" but was "tasked" with making recommendations to the HPC Council. Mr Seale defined this more clearly at the Confer Conference in London in January 2010, when he said "we invite them in to do a job, they do it, then we say goodbye". In spite of the clarity of this message, many people continued to believe that the HPC could only regulate the practice if it paid due attention to the reality of the work as it was currently functioning, which would require it to establish a relationship with the field which both recognized and was responsible for the actual practice. In fact, this is not the case. Professor Annie Turner was the most persistent HPC member to transmit this knowledge to the professionals. In one PLG meeting after another she told the members that they were not being asked to come up with standards that reflected the work currently done, but to come up with standards that the HPC could accommodate within its established framework of regulation. She glossed this as an opportunity to change the profession and bring it into the 21st century. This is a beautifully clear example that the HPC Council knew what it was doing (no one disagreed with her or tried to prevent her from repeating her advice as the months rolled into years). Not only was it encouraging a select few (selected by the HPC, not the profession) to change the basis upon which the practice operated, it also advanced an "enlightened rationale" that standards should take their reference not from real-life practice, but from utopian images held by the HPC of the 21st century. As a kind of cruel twist, the HPC not only invited the PLG to come up with these imaginary standards, but constructed the context of its work in such a way as to make it impossible to achieve. The standards were still not complete even after double time was allowed.

To give you a clearer idea of what I mean, here's an example from the first meeting of the PLG. The participants are seated in the same room that Dr Cross's case will later be heard. The tables and chairs are in the same format. The power is in the same place—upstage along the short side of the oblong. A wooden gavel sits in front of Di Waller, who acts as the Chair of the meeting. The first moment of closure was triggered when Brian Magee asked if the PLG would be free to decide that regulation would not be in the service users' interest. Di Waller responded by suggesting that it was a good time to break for lunch. After lunch Magee's point was not mentioned again.

A second moment arose out of two contentious issues: the skewed representation of the PLG and the difficulties raised by many of the texts received from the call for ideas. It was noted that this was the first time that a professional body was entering the process without having applied of its own accord (all the main bodies having publicly declared that the HPC was an inappropriate regulator for the field), and Dr van der Gaag said that it was not, therefore, necessary that this group process should meet the HPC's own criteria for advancement. Dissension was voiced and the meeting became tense—if these criteria weren't being applied, which criteria would be, and on whose says so? Professor Waller tried to keep things moving by saying that the group should get on with the work themselves, otherwise the government would "do it to them". Professor Fonagy endorsed this "wholeheartedly", adding that the group should not waste time considering arguments that were not related to "the protection of the public". Kathi Murphy replied that the protection of the public is important to the vast majority of practitioners and that she had never met anyone who was against this principle, but the principle may be understood very differently by different people—i.e., what exactly, does this mean? Professor Lucas stressed the importance of engaging with the opposition and trying to understand their arguments, yet he was baffled as to why some people thought that HPC "regulation would lower current standards". Other members agreed that the group should engage with what they called the opposition (i.e., those not invited to sit on the HPC), and asked how this could be done given that there was no representation from those groups on the PLG. On this difficult point, and although time had been allocated until 3:30, the meeting was suddenly brought to a close at 1:30 pm.

The second meeting of this group was planned for the end of January 2009. By this time, a long, detailed, and carefully written letter had been sent to all the members from one of the groups excluded from the proceedings. The letter set out a number of important points very clearly making it possible for the PLG to engage with "the opposition" even though "it wasn't in the room". This engagement was conducted according to the best "Yes, minister" principles, and led to absolutely no discussion whatsoever of the points that were raised in the letter. The letter was kicked into the long grass with a couple of mentions of "public protection" and Di Waller's clarion call to "keep it vague", and just "make a sketch". Nevertheless, on day two of this particular meeting, the agenda required the group to address some of the problems raised by the call for ideas. Michael Guthrie had reduced the scope and variety of arguments made against HPC regulation for the field into a few lines headed "conscientious objection" (a phrase used by only a few correspondents as a last ditch attempt to persuade the HPC to acknowledge the numbers of people who would not, in good conscience, be able to join the HPC register).

- The Register should be structured to provide for a list of "conscientious objectors". A list of "non-licensed", "non-certified" psychotherapists exists in the US State of Vermont.
- The PLG may wish to consider whether such an approach would be meaningful to either members of the public or the profession and achieve the public protection aims of statutory regulation. No known arrangement similar to that in Vermont exists in professional regulation in the UK.

What follows is a sketch of what happened in the discussion. I wrote down everything that I could in the order that it was said, noting names of who said what. It is not exactly verbatim, but I think it is a fair record of the discussion (it has been posted on the hpcwatchdog.blogspot, which is read by many PLG members, and no one approached me to correct it). The VOICE indicates someone whose name I did not connect with the comment at the time. Voices off are interjections from one or two people in the public gallery. Look out for the way that Di Waller manages to cut the discussion with a promise to return which she promptly breaks. Note also when Julian Lousada points out that they've "parked" a difficult issue she replies publicly that she is not worried, because they will "be seen" to have gone through the motion of debate. Here it is:

Mick Cooper:	Is Principled Non Compliance a practical option in your opinion?
Michael Guthrie:	I cannot foresee the government being able to accommodate it.
Brian Magee:	There is a possibility of several different registers springing up all simultaneously with HPC—have you thought of that?
Michael Guthrie:	[nonplussed]
Mary Clark-Glass:	I've looked carefully at the arguments—that people choose willingly to go private and so on. But that's the same with dentists, and they can do a lot of damage, or estate agents—they can rob you blind. If you are in a position where someone comes to you and you can do harm, then, well, I'm afraid I cannot support it.
Annie Turner:	Why are they asking the regulator to hold their names on the register if they don't want to register and be regulated? You can't have your cake and eat it too you know.
Nick Turner:	Are they the registered non-registered?
Jonathon Coe:	What is the purpose of regulation? Without statutory regulation people who are known to be harmful will continue to practise. People need to be prevented from practising. Either it is the regulator or the law, and the law can't be different for one person than another.
Peter Fonagy:	They could get taken off the Non-Register.
Nick Turner:	Or sent to Vermont (laughter).
Julian Lousada:	We must not ridicule them—they hold their position seriously, and hold it well.
Jonathon Coe:	Not ridicule, but put the facts. The evidence base is clear that there is harm. Best outcome of this process is the vast majority will continue to practise in the way they've done before, but bad practitioners will be removed. We have to come back again and again and again to the public protection issues.

| | We are in a new world now. Professional-led self-regulation is dead. The Health & Social Care Bill last year said there must be an equal number of lay people on the board as professionals. |

Peter Fonagy: I totally agree. These people—we should take a very firm view. Compared to other professions, psychotherapy is definitely potentially harmful. Five per cent of practitioners cause damage.
[voices off: what is the source of this statistic? etc.]
... The public is ill-served, the present situation is ineffective. We hope it will become more evidence based. A little bit more notice of what is known in general will lead to an improvement in client care. Registration is not new. The medical profession was against regulation. It is an urgent issue for public protection.

Linda Matthews: We should not mock or ridicule these people. But the public needs protection and therefore we need regulation. Professionals need protection too. I think it is a good move for the profession.

Julian Lousda: We are a victim of our own rhetoric. Public protection—we are part of the public, the clinical community is part of the public. Care providers are vulnerable. The public is at risk from us, yes, but we are vulnerable to them too!

Carmen Ablack: It is a philosophical position that these people are taking. It's not about a "them", there are several different groups. I would not choose the HPC if I had any choice.

Jeff Lucas: Other aspirant groups have had this problem.

Di Waller (Chair):   We have all been lobbied, let's be frank, but the letter is philosophical. They point to the confusion between state and statutory regulation, and raise the question of totalitarianism. [sigh] Look, I've lived in an eastern bloc country, oh, for many years, I know what totalitarianism is, and this is not that. It might look like it from the outside, but it doesn't feel like it inside the HPC. Also they talk of the medical model ... No, no [shakes her head slowly from side to side] oh dear ...

Fiona Ballantine Dykes:	We must take this seriously. They have a petition, and it had 1,600 names on it at the beginning of the week, a lot of names on it that I respect. I'm not willingly part of this process. Perhaps I am willingly dragged into it, but only because I believe I decided I had to join in order to try to influence it.
Voice:	The HPC gives public protection. It protects the registrant. It helps with credibility. There is really nothing to do but pay the fee and gain status and credibility.
Mary Clark-Glass:	And upholding public confidence. It's a matter of pride to have been recognised by the HPC, to get external validation.
Di Waller:	Oo, things are getting a little bit heated. Shall we take a short ten minute break and come back to finish it off? … [they break up for ten minutes, then reconvene]
Di Waller:	Right, now, we need to move on.
Michael Guthrie:	Which protected titles do you want to have? We protect titles, rather than function, but we have to police mis-use of title, and we do that through the "intention to deceive". If people don't register, we won't have public protection.
Carmen Ablack:	Registered counsellor, ok, but what about a registered life coach? We need to look after, preserve, make clear, how to deal with the widespread use of the word.
Mary Clark-Glass:	If we think it's right, we'll do it, and ignore what goes on elsewhere.
Carmen Ablack:	If they are not doing it well enough, and they are using my professional title …
Mary Clark-Glass:	We'll get them on 'if you go beyond your skills and competence'. Prevention is the better protection of the public.
Julian Lousada:	We've parked a difficult issue.
Di Waller:	But we can be seen to have done justice to the question.

No authentic evidence has ever been produced to substantiate the apparent facts paraded by members of the PLG that are reported here. With such an auspicious beginning it should come as no surprise that when the final proposals of this group were subjected to the public consultation an unprecedented 1,100 replies were received (October 2009) (many texts arguing against this form of regulation for the field have been published, see for example Postle, 2007; Parker & Revelli, 2008; Maresfield Report, 2009, McGovern, Fischer, Ferlie & Exworthy, 2009; Reeves & Mollon, 2009; etc.). But the HPC is tenacious, and Michael Guthrie managed to massage these replies into a report which allowed the CEO to persuade the Council to allow him to write to the Secretary of State recommending the machinery should proceed to legislation. The meeting at which this sleight of hand was achieved was the Council meeting of 10 December, 2009.

At that meeting Mary Clark-Glass acknowledged the huge differences in responses to the public consultation, the disparity in the field, and the upset that is evident from so many of the responders, and even said that she found "great interest in the disputing stances" before concluding "but we must go ahead because of public protection".

Deep Sagar asked: "Would it be fair to assume that we did not make the distinction between whether people were in favour of regulation rather than specifically HPC regulation?" but failed to make any capital out of the reply (which was "yes").

Keith Ross (HPC Council member since 2001) ignored the content and praised the *process* of feedback: "It highlights the value of consultation".

Julia Drown (a new Council member and a former Labour MP) said, somewhat confusingly, "We need to do further work on what is meant by the clear messages we have got".

Jeff Lucas said "It is a balanced report" before adding "I accept that we have more work to do on this".

Annie Turner repeated "It is a balanced report" and then added her rather sinister observation that "concerns are not new for any profession coming onto the register, but they usually soon disappear".

Mr Seale said a Section 60 was uncontroversial (this is the legislation that is required to pass the practitioners onto the register) which provoked a ripple of laughter (which at least recognized that there was contention on precisely this point), then added that in his opinion the PLG would have more work to do now than it had during the previous year. This seemed to suggest that the work done by the PLG so far had in fact put the HPC further back than they were at the beginning of the process. This is rather strong evidence that the field presents significant problems for the HPC and adds weight to all those who argue against the HPC model of regulation for the field. However, this inconvenient truth was buried when Jeff Lucas opened up the blame game. He said the problems could be pinned on the "advanced practitioners" (a twist on the "old boy" rhetoric) who couldn't or *wouldn't* grasp the concept of *threshold-level entry*; they had consistently blocked progress, he said. Mary Clark-Glass acknowledged that they had struggled, adding "though clearly not enough". Julia Drown, perhaps to show that she was keen, said that she could see the complexity of HPC regulation in this field and then, without giving any reasons or evidence for her certainty (which verges on the reckless), said she was sure that "we can do it". This prompted Anna van der Gaag to try to conclude with "I think that I am hearing from you that you see the need for further work. You see the need for the PLG to help us make the right decision to take the work forward. We do want the PLG to continue". She had jumped the gun, because Eileen Thornton said: "If we are going ahead with the PLG, what about its membership? We need to reflect the disturbances that have been raised". "Yes, absolutely," said Anna, a phrase that was to reveal its true meaning in time, as the PLG reconvened some time later with exactly the same membership.

Mr Seale talked about the problems involved in multiple-register transfer—from an IT point of view, the data was very dirty, and time would certainly be needed to clean it all up before opening the register. It was precisely at this moment that the meeting noticed that the IT expert had left the room. Michael Guthrie, keen to keep things moving, leapt into the breach and said: "I think there is an algorithm followed by a manual process". The lack of reality continued when Mr Seale raised the question of the grand-parenting period, saying it should be extended from two to three years "because a lot of people leave it to the last moment". Julia Drown said "That's not the right reason!" Mr Seale shrugged and smiled, and the Council agreed to his proposal.

This left a very little time for a discussion about the highly controversial generic standards. These standards are supposed to be the central strut of HPC strategy and crucial for "protecting the public". They were heavily criticized both by the Psychologists and Psychotherapists and Councillors, and had therefore been hastily changed.

Eileen Thornton said that the PLG process had made quite significant *changes* to the wording and that the amended document was now with the original 12 bodies. Anna van der Gaag corrected her: it was a significant positive *impact*. Diane Waller said, somewhat wearily, that some professions had not been very happy with the *language* of these standards for quite a while. Her own profession, the drama therapists, had admitted that they never considered the generic standards as relevant to them at all! This extraordinary admission was recorded in the documentation accompanying the previous Council meeting but seems to have raised no eyebrows. She was pleased that they were now being "positively *impacted*". Eileen Thornton (chair of the education and training committee) concluded by saying they were also revisiting the SET 1 (standards of education and training), where problems were constantly arising. She added that these problems were expected to continue as the HPC "spread out to different kinds of registrant". This clear warning raised no further discussion whatsoever at the meeting and Dr van der Gaag concluded by saying: "I think that what I've heard is that you recommend … further work, further consultation, and further discussion. You wish to involve the PLG in that ongoing work, and you have not identified any specific issues to prevent us from regulating psychotherapy and counselling".

Jonathan Bracken (solicitor and parliamentary consultant to the HPC) was grinning very widely indeed when he said "you are making a clear decision that you are capable, but further work needs to be done". *You*, mark you, not "we".

One year later, 10 December, 2010, the High Court upheld the right of a group of psychoanalytic organizations (known as the PsyReg group and amongst whose members were those whose letter had been so significantly ignored at the second PLG meeting) to go ahead with a judicial review of the HPC. The group aimed its attack at the heart of the problem in an attempt to hold the HPC to account and to remind it that it is not above the law. On a more tactical level, the action aimed to reveal the duplicity of the HPC, and to show the government (which by now had changed from Labour to the Conservative and Liberal Democrat coalition) that the HPC's word could not be relied upon.

The High Court (the case was heard in the Royal Courts of Justice; the transcript of this hearing is available from the website of the College of Psychoanalysts-UK) is a quite different realm of law from the HPC. There was also a quite different attitude. On entering the building, you don't even have to give your name. There is no tag to wear, and you are trusted to find your own way around and to know how to behave. You aren't subjected to the administrator's whim, you are not locked into a decompression chamber and you can work out the rules quite easily because they have years of tradition behind them and actually make sense.

The upshot of this hearing was to establish that the HPC had been charged in a Government White Paper of 2007 with assessing (a) the regulatory needs of counselling and psychotherapy and (b) whether its own system was capable of accommodating this field. However, instead of assessing its capability, and instead of paying attention to the problems raised by many different constituencies in the field, the HPC proceeded *as if* its suitability and capacity were a foregone conclusion (the idea that the government might be granting them a licence to print money seems to have gotten in the way of any duty to act thoughtfully). The question of what, exactly, it means to regulate is posed right here. The HPC acts as if regulating requires it simply to hold names on a database and to be equipped to hold FTP hearings (the question of its role in regulating training and education is, as ever, occluded). Mr Justice Burton summed up this stance quite nicely—"are there enough buildings and photocopiers". This may well be what regulation means to the HPC, but for anyone genuinely concerned with the real regulation of a practice it looks like little more than an image which distracts the unwary from the illogical and irrational goings-on behind the scenes.

Within a few weeks of the hearing (which upheld the right of the PsyReg group to go ahead with a Judicial Review of the HPC), the government announced its strategy for regulating healthcare workers, social workers, and social care workers (16 February 2011). The new direction effectively called a halt to the HPC's hopes of capturing the counsellors and psychotherapists and proposed changes to the regulatory landscape which will give new names and different powers to the existing bodies; there is even some talk of injecting competition into the regulatory field! However, the ideology that gives rise to these kinds of regulatory regimes is still very much alive and the situation in which our economy and our educational and health care system currently find themselves does not bode well for enlightened and rational future prospects.

We've been considering modern regulation in action, not from what people say about it, but from what they actually do. What has emerged is a view of regulatory inaction where regulation in its true sense (i.e., to sustain a real practice and not just the superficial behaviour of its practitioners) is weakened and something else—a simulacrum of expertise—is put in its place. In what was once a carefully managed space, in the hands of people with knowledge and responsibility for the actual practice, there is now a crowd of others—politicians, administrators, lay people, and lawyers—all jostling to exploit an opportunity for their own ends and advantages.

REFERENCES

Atkins, C., Bee, S. & Button, F. (2007). *Taking Liberties*. London: Revolver Books.

Braverman, H. (1976). *Labor and Monopoly Capital: The Degradation of Work in the Twentieth Century*. USA: Monthly Review Press.

Carr-Saunders, P. & Wilson, P. (1933). *The Professions*. Oxford: Clarendon Press.

Cooper, A. (2001). The state of mind we're in: Social anxiety, governance and the audit society. *Psychoanalytic Studies*, 3(3–4): 349–362.

Docherty, T. (2008). *The English Question, or Academic Freedom*. Eastbourne: Sussex Academic Press.

Durkheim, E. (1957). *Professional Ethics and Civic Morals*. London: Routledge.

Eagleton, T. (2011). The death of universities. Academia has become a servant of the status quo. Its malaise runs so much deeper than tuition fees. *The Guardian Newspaper*, Comment. 18 December: Main Section, p. 43, and online at http://www.guardian.co.uk/commentisfree/2010/dec/17/death-universities-malaise-tuition-fees

Fish, S. (2010). The value of higher education made literal. *The New York Times*, Opinionator, 13 December. http://opinionator.blogs.nytimes.com/2010/12/13/the-value-of-higher-education-made-literal/

Freidson, E. (2001). *Professionalism: The Third Logic*. Cambridge: Polity Press.

Gerstmann, E. & Streb, M. J. (2006). *Academic Freedom at the Dawn of a New Century: How Terrorism, Governments, and Culture Wars Impact Free Speech*. Stanford: Stanford University Press.

Gombrich, R. (2000) Graduate Institute of Policy Studies (GRIPS) in Tokyo in 2000 ("British Higher Education Policy in the Last Twenty Years: The Murder of a Profession").

Haines, F. (2011). *The Paradox of Regulation: What Regulation Can Achieve and What it Cannot Achieve*. Cheltenham: Edward Elgar.

Hansard: Health Professions Order (2001). Debate in House of Commons Committee: http://www.publications.parliament.uk/pa/cm200102/cmstand/deleg4/st011126/11126s05.htm

Head, S. (2011). *The Grim Threat to British Universities*. New York, NY: The New York Review of Books, Jan 13.

House of Commons vote: http://www.publications.parliament.uk/pa/cm200102/cmhansrd/vo011128/debtext/11128-28.htm. Approval in the House of Lords: http://www.publications.parliament.uk/pa/ld200102/ldhansrd/vo011213/text/11213-26.htm#11213-26_head

Johnston, P. (2010). *Bad Laws: An Explosive Analysis of Britain's Petty Rules, Health and Safety Lunacies and Madcap Laws*. London: Constable Robin.

Kennedy, I. (1981). *The Unmasking of Medicine (based on his BBC Reith Lectures)*. London: George Allen & Unwin.

Kennedy, I., Howard, R., Jarman, B. & Mclean, M. (2001). Learning from Bristol: The report of the public inquiry into children's heart surgery at the Bristol Royal Infirmary 1984–1995. London: HMSO.

Khurana, R. (2007). *From Higher Aims to Hired Hands: the Social Transformation of American Business Schools and the Unfulfilled Promise of Management as a Profession*. Princeton: Princeton University Press.

King, L. & Moutsou, C. (Eds) (2010). *Rethinking Audit Cultures: A Critical Look at Evidence-based Practice in Psychotherapy and Beyond*. Ross-on-Wye: PCCS Books.

Leader, D. (2008). *Psychoanalysis and Regulation*. In: Parker & Revelli (Eds.). pp. 205–216.

Maresfield Report on the regulation of psychotherapy in the UK. London 2009.

McGovern, G., Fischer, M., Ferlie, E. & Exworthy, M. (2009). *Statutory regulation and the future of professional practice in psychotherapy and counselling: evidence from the field*. Report from the Department of Management, King's College London.

Medical Auxiliaries. *The Times (London)*, 30 November 1959.

Mills, C. W. (1959). *The Sociological Imagination*. New York: Oxford University Press.

Morley, M., Court, D. & Tuck, J. P. (1959). Speech Therapy, Letter to the Editor, *The Times (London)*, 30 November 1959.

Naylor, R. (2007). *Whose Degree Is It Anyway? Why, How and Where Universities Are Failing Our Students*. GB: Pencil Sharp.

O'Neill, O. (2002). *A Question of Trust. BBC Reith Lectures*. Cambridge: Cambridge University Press.

Parker, I. & Revelli, S. (Eds.) (2008). *Psychoanalytic Practice and State Regulation*. London: Karnac.

Postle, D. (2007). *Regulating the Psychological Therapies: from taxonomy to taxidermy*. Ross-on-Wye: PCCS Books.

Power, M. (1994). *The Audit Explosion*. Paper No 7. London: Demos.

Power, M. (1997). *The Audit Society: Rituals of Verification*. Oxford: Oxford University Press.

Power, M. (2009). Performance and the logic of the audit trail. Hurly-Burly, 1: 193–201.

Raab, D. (2009). *The Assault on Liberty: What Went Wrong with Rights*. London: Fourth Estate.

Reeves, R. & Mollon, P. (2009). The state regulation of psychotherapy: from self-regulation to self-mutilation? *Attachment: New Directions in Psychotherapy and Relational Psychoanalysis*, 3: 1–19.

Registers for Eight Professions In Medicine Under Bill. *The Times (London)*, 20 November 1959.

Russell, C. (1993). *Academic Freedom*. London: Routledge.

Sanders, C. (2000). New body may feel old pains. *Times Higher Education Supplement*. 4 Feb. http://www.timeshighereducation.co.uk/story.asp?storycode=150040

Scott, B. (2009). A case of dialectical disease: A tale of a Health Professions Council fitness to practice hearing of a psychologist. Guest Blog post 20 March: http://hpcwatchdog.blogspot.com/2010/03/guest-post-by-bruce-scott-on-ftp.html

Scott, J. C. (1998). *Seeing Like a State: How Certain Schemes to Improve the Human Condition have Failed*. Yale University Press.

Smith, J. (2001). *The Shipman Inquiry*. London: HMSO.

Snell, R. (2009). Some thoughts on the Audit Culture and how to survive it. *Hurly-Burly* 1: 203–208.

Strathern, M. (Ed.) (2000). *Audit Cultures: Anthropological Studies in Accountability, Ethics and the Academy*. Abingdon: Routledge.

The regulation of health professions: report of a review of the Professions Supplementary to Medicine Act (1960) with recommendations for new legislation. April 1996. JM Consulting Ltd, Bristol BS8 4EJ.

Travers, M. (2007). *The New Bureaucracy: Quality Assurance and Its Critics*. Bristol: Policy Press.

Trust, Assurance, and Safety—The regulation of Health Professionals in the 21st Century (2007). Government White Paper. London: HMSO.

Voruz, V. (2009). Security is the new freedom. *Hurly-Burly*, 1: 221–226.

Wolf, A. (2008). War of the professions. *Analysis*. BBC Radio 4. 24 April 2008.

INDEX